New
PIRATES AND

This book is dedicated to the you......... .... of my own pirate crew, as shown below. Steven Ellis Cahill is the little pirate on the right. He, with my three other offspring, robbed me of my meager fortune and forced me, under extreme verbal abuse, to lead them from New England into tropical Florida, where they merrily joined Walt Disney's "Pirates of the Caribbean," allowing me to escape their greedy clutches two weeks later, to return home pennyless.

Cover Photos: ISBN 0916787-13-3

Pirate ship rounding the cliffs of Maine, from the movie, *"The Sea Hawk,"* photo courtesy Peabody Museum, Salem, MA. Pirates aboard ship prepare to attack, photo from the film, *"The Black Pirate,"* courtesy Peabody Museum, Salem, MA. Illustration of pirate by famed artist Howard Pyle; Painting of pirate chief Sam Bellamy, captain of the galley **WHYDAH**, which sank off Cape Cod in 1717, by Trish Cahill; Al Jenard, noted metal detecting expert of New Durham, New Hampshire, hunting for treasure at Plum Island, MA; Author Bob Cahill, with Gil Arrington of Marblehead, and Tom Hubbell of Springfield, MA., enter pirate cave on Grand Cayman Island, West Indies, where Hubbell found a pirate sword and a chest of Spanish silver coins; Background photo of silver coins, gold, and other treasure, recently found off Wellfleet, MA by Barry Clifford of Orleans, Cape Cod, photo courtesy of Barry Clifford.

Printed in Canada

INTRODUCTION

Pirates were roaming the New England Coast at least ten years before the Pilgrims first settled at Plymouth. Peter Easton, one of England's most notorious pirates in 1610, boasted of having almost 1,000 men and forty ships under his command. With ten of these pirate vessels, he raided the fishermen of Newfoundland and Nova Scotia in 1612. Two years later, pirate Henry Mainwaring attacked Newfoundland with some 300 men and eight vessels. The King of England later pardoned Henry and hired him as commander of an English fleet to attack Barbary pirates off the coast of Africa.

Pay for the average seaman in the English Navy was poor, as was the food on naval ships. Sailors prefered shipping out on fishing boats, merchant ships, and privateers. Except for privateering, a seaman had no opportunity to make himself a small fortune— whereas in pirating, a mariner might retire in comfort after a couple of years at sea.

In the early 1600s, England had over 500 privateers sailing the high seas, attacking and plundering enemy vessels, the captains and crews keeping much of the loot for themselves. King James recalled them all— offering, *"peace with all nations,"* in 1607. The King also imposed the law that *"no English sailors shall be employed on foreign ships."* Though his *"peace-proposal"* didn't last very long, nearly all England's privateersmen went into the lucrative occupation of pirating.

New England's first English explorer, John Smith, who admitted he came here *"searching for gold,"* said in 1614, *"not having true payment for seamen, they cannot live without means, but necessity will force them to steale; and when they are once entered into that trade, they are hardly reclaimed... Privateers in time of war are a nursery for pirates against a peace."*

Spain, after discovering gold, emerald, and silver mines in Central and South America, controlled most of the islands of the Caribbean, but by 1630, Englishmen had settled on the Caribbean Islands of Tortuga and Barbadoes. England also controlled Bermuda in the Atlantic, by which Spanish galleons loaded with treasure had to pass on their way home to Spain. They were prey for privateersmen and pirates. The French had settled on the island of Hispaniola, also near the Spanish trade route. These French settlers were called *"Buccaneers,"* because they smoked their meat over open campfires. They were also known for their daring in attacking Spanish treasure ships. In little open boats, they waited at night for treasure galleons to pass, and sinking their own boats, they would board the galleons. Leaving themselves no means of escape, they would fight furiously to take over the ship, or die. They often soaked themselves in cow's blood to frighten the pantaloons off the Spanish sailors, who, if they survived, swore that they were *"attacked by devils."*

There were also many pirates roaming the North Atlantic, Mediterranean, Red Sea and Indian Ocean, in constant search of Arab and Indian vessels filled with rich cargoes. The new little settlements cropping up in New England, many of them populated with *"thieves, criminals and vagrants sent as slaves and servants,"* traded for food and merchandise in all the seas of the world. Therefore, it's little wonder that most 17th and 18th century pirates were New Englanders. This little book is about them, with as many clues available as to where they stashed their unclaimed treasures, and what has been uncovered thus-far. There is good reason why most of the notorious buccaneers buried their riches here, and not on foreign soil — read on, and maybe you'll reap where they have sown.

Bob Cahill

"The Buccaneers," a painting by Frederick Waugh, now in the Brockton Library, is owned by Vose Galleries in Boston. Coincidentally, Mr. Vose, founder of the Galleries, discovered part of Captain Kidd's treasure buried under his house in Jamestown, Rhode Island.

I
A LITTLE MAINE BULL AND THE HOLY GHOST

New England's first official pirate was Dixie Bull, a quiet trader in beaver skins, who was forced into becoming a sea-robber when he was attacked by French pirates who took his *"coats, rugs, blankets, and biskets,"* leaving him destitute at Penobscot, Maine, in June of 1632. Dixie was furious to say the least, and he got sixteen other Maine settlers to join him in pursuit of the French to get his possessions back, but searching the coast for two weeks, they couldn't find the French pirate ship. Frustrated, Dixie decided to go after English trading vessels instead. He also attacked New England fishermen in his little pirate shallop, and forced them to join his newly established pirate gang. Then, in a bold manuever he landed at Pemaquid and attacked the little settlement there, stealing some 500 pounds sterling in merchandise. As he was sailing off with his booty, some of the settlers shot at his shallop and killed one of his men.

Next, he went after Captain Anthony Dike of Salem, who with four others, was fur trading with the Indians along the coast of Maine. Dike, his men and his ship were captured by Bull and his pirate crew, and their furs were confiscated. One of the pirate crew, Dike later reported, *"was fearful that if caught, would all be hanged."* Dike's crewmen, Smith, Johnson, Conant, and Palfrey, were let go, but Dixie Bull kidnapped Dike, who was an experienced navigator. He threatened to kill Dike if he didn't lead the pirates to Virginia. Apparently Bull realized that his crew was becoming a bit squeemish, and he wanted to take them out of New England waters. Dike, however, refused to be the pilot for these pirates, and Bull reneged on his word, finally allowing Dike to go free.

In the meantime, Captain Walter Neal of Portsmouth, New Hampshire, (then called Piscataqua), sent word to Governor John Winthrop at Boston, that he needed *"an armed pinnace to lead an expedition against Bull."* The Governor complied, and sent Sam Maverick with twenty men in an armed ship to Portsmouth. Joined by four New Hampshire vessels, this first official New England naval fleet searched the coast of Maine for Bull and his pirates, but after two months at sea, found no trace of them. Three deserters from Bull's crew were rounded up on the mainland in Maine and brought to Boston in chains, where they were interrogated by the Governor. *"Dixie Bull has joined the French,"* one of the crewmen said. *"Bull has gone to England,"* testified another. About that same time, Governor Winthrop received a hand-delivered message from one of Dixie's crewmen, which read: *"I will cause you no more problems. I am heading South — Dixie Bull."* True to his word, the Governor had no more problems from Dixie Bull, and the next heard of him in Boston, was a poem, written in London that made its way to Boston two years later. The first line was, *"Pirates, your flag and anchor pull, for Curtis killed your Dixie Bull . ."* Apparently Dixie had gone to England, and at Bristol, so the poem declared, *"was killed in a sword fight with one Daniel Curtis."* So New England's first pirate was killed in a duel, unless of course, Dixie Bull wrote the poem and sent it to Governor Winthrop, in order to cover his tracks.

There was always a fine line between piracy and privateering, the later often called *"official piracy,"* when a nation, colony, or state, designated certain ships and commanders, under a *"letter-of marquis,"* to search out, destroy and confiscate the cargo of any enemy vessel. Many privateersmen, especially from Massachusetts and Rhode Island, left ports as privateersmen, turned pirate, and returned home secretly to hide their ill-gotten goods. One Captain Thomas Hawkins of Boston, with a commission from the Massachusetts General Court, sailed as a privateersman to Spain on November 12, 1644 in the 40-ton **SEAFORTH,** as did Captain Thomas Bredcake *"to Algeria to take Turkish pirates who attack our fish traders off Spain."* A vague cloud of doubt hung in the Boston air when they returned, as to whether they just took *"enemy and pirate vessels during their expeditions, or ships of ours as well,"* notes Governor Bradford of Plymouth. Hawkins' grandson was later tried in Boston as a pirate, and Bradford says of both crews, *"they distempered themselves with drink and were like madmen."* Another privateersman, Thomas Cromwell, commissioned in 1645, brought a prize enemy ship back from the West Indies and turned it over to Governor Winthrop, but Bradford considered Cromwell a pirate too, for he and his crew loosely spent Spanish gold, *"ill-gotten,"* in Plymouth pubs, before sailing on to Boston. Another so-called privateersman was Captain Edward Hull of the barque **SWALLOW.** He successfully captured French and Dutch vessels and returned to Boston a wealthy man in 1653, but on the way home, he stopped at Block Island off Rhode Island and robbed the home of Captain Sebada of over 100 pounds sterling. Hull, deemed a pirate, soon sailed to England to avoid the hangman. Captain Hull's brother John was the first to mint New England's famed pinetree shillings, and a famed descendant of his was Isaac Hull, heroic commander of — the **U.S.F. CONSTITUTION,** during the War of 1812.

Another great American naval hero, Admiral "Bull" Halsey of

World War II fame, also had a notorious pirate commander as an ancestor. John Halsey, was made commander of the privateer **CHARLES** at Boston in 1693, when he was only 23 years old. He did chase after French pirates off Nova Scotia for awhile, but then, with the blessing of his crew, sailed for the Red Sea to attack and loot rich Indian and Arab vessels. After accumulating some $200,000 in treasure, he fell ill at Madagascar and died. Most of his crew returned home richer for the experience.

The same year Hull returned to Boston, 1653, another pirate, Captain Robert Harding, came into that same port with a captured prize, **THE HOLY GHOST**. Harding was a good friend of Governor Winthrop's, and in fact, had sailed with him from England in the **EAGLE** to help settle Salem in 1630. *"The Council* (Governor's Council) *invited the Captain and company of the ship to come into Boston Harbor,"* wrote Edward Rawson, the Governor's secretary. *"the ship and company faling upon the coast of New England were in great extremity, wanting provisions... The Captain coming ashore, as also some of the Company, they were imprisoned...".* The **HOLY GHOST** was a Spanish ship taken by Harding and his Dutch crew off Barbadoes, and according to Governor Searle of Barbadoes, *"was taken by pirates."* In a letter to the Massachusetts Council, Governor Searle wrote, *"we request your assistance for stoping the ship. We have lately understood these robbers by fained pretenses and discourses, to colour their action, have endeavard to shelter themselves under your authority in New England."* Searle suggested that the Massachusetts Governor send the pirates back to him in chains, along with the treasure the ship carried. The Massachusetts Governor's Council decided not to ship the pirates back to the West Indies, but instead, the pirates were released from jail. *"There was no one to bear evidence against Captain Harding and his Company,"* the Council concluded. Yet, four months later, October 10, 1653, mariner Mathew Hill of Boston swore a deposition that, *"two Spaniards had leaped overboard from the HEYLY GHEEST and were picked up by me in my ship off Barbadoes, and another ship had picked up six Spanish sailors from that ship. The Spanish reported that there was a chest of gold dust six foot long, and another chest of jewels and pearls and seven hogheads of pieces-of-eight was in said ship."* Two of Mathew Hill's men, Frances Blackman and John Dukley, confirmed Hill's statement.

The **HOLY GHOST**, renamed the **HAPPY ENTRANCE**, was now docked at Salem, Massachusetts, and the Governor sent constables there to *"have the whole cargo of goods brought ashore, that* *there might be true invoice taken thereof, because it was reported to be a vessel of great treasury."* There was no treasure found aboard at Salem, but it must be noted that Captain Harding had sailed his ship to the Damariscotta River and the Pemaquid settlement in Maine, before docking at Salem. The Governor had no reason to hold Harding, his men, or the ship, which Harding insisted was not Spanish but Dutch. He left Salem and sailed to Nova Scotia, where he sold the **HAPPY ENTRANCE**, ex **HOLY GHOST**, and was not heard from again. What happened to the chests of gold dust and jewels and the seven large barrels of Spanish silver coins? You don't suppose Captain Harding paid off those Boston politicians to let him go, do you? There is strong historical evidence that in the late 17th and early 18th centuries, when piracy was at its zenith, bold buccaneers in great numbers came to New England to stash their booty, mainly because Our Founding Fathers, leaders of a God fearing puritanical society, were at the docks to greet them — with their hands out.

The Earl of Bellomont, Governor of Massachusetts, New Hampshire, and New York, who was also Captain Kidd's partner. This portrait of Captain Kidd (right) was painted while he awaited execution. The piece of cloth attached to it in the left lower corner is from his coat, and the frame is made from the planks of his ship ADVENTURE GALLEY, courtesy Maritime Museum, London.

II
RHODE ISLAND RENEGADES

Most New England pirates started out as privateersmen, hired by local merchants and commissioned by one of the Colonies, to search out and destroy enemy shipping and to confiscate any cargoes going to and from enemy ports. At various times during the late 1600s and throughout the early 1700s, England and America were at war with France, Spain, Holland and Portugal. Spain and England signed a peace treaty in 1668, yet in Rhode Island, privateering commissions against the Spanish of the West Indies were not repealed until 1672. Even then, New England privateersmen continued to attack Spanish treasure ships on *"the Spanish Main,"* sailing from Central America to Spain. Noted English pirate Henry Morgan, who always considered himself a privateersman, sacked the wealthy Spanish port of Puerto Velo, in 1668 and, with 1,200 men, attacked and captured Panama in 1671, confiscating millions of dollars in gold and silver. King Charles II knighted him and made him Governor of Jamaica. England and France were at war from 1689 to September 1697, and then waged war again for almost fifty years over the Spanish succession. Many privateersmen after putting to sea in 1696 and 97, and capturing French ships, returned to home port months later to discover that America was no longer at war with that country and that, because of their ignorance, they were considered pirates. Some privateersmen, however, were intent on piracy from the moment they left port, and would attack other vessels no matter what flag they flew.

Cotton Mather, leading New England religious leader of the day, insisted that, *"privateering easily degenerates into the piratical; and the privateering trade is usually carried on with unchristian temper, and proves an inlet unto much debauchery and iniquity."* When the crew of the privateer **ANTONIO** mutinied, set the captain and officers adrift in a rowboat in mid-Atlantic, and took up piracy, Mather cherished the incident as an example of God's intervention into this *"debauchery and iniquity."* The **ANTONIO** sailed into Charlestown, Massachusetts in June of 1672, *"and by a surprising Providence of God,"* says Mather, *"the Master and his afflicted Company in the long-boat, also arrived at Charlestown."* The **ANTONIO** pirates fled to the home of a Major Nicholas Shapleigh, where they were given shelter. *"Alas, the pirates were apprehended,"* says Mather, *"and the ringleaders of this murderous piracy, John Smith, William Forrest, and Alexander Wilson, had sentence of death executed on them in Boston."* Major Shapleigh however, an upright citizen of Charlestown, was only fined for harboring the culprits.

Two years later, the Dutch privateer **FLYING HORSE**, Jurrian Aernouts commander, was attacking merchantmen and fishing sloops off Block Island. One captured fisherman finally told Aernouts that the war between the English and Dutch was over, so he sailed into Boston and was warmly greeted. There, he hired merchant John Rhoade to assist him in attacking French vessels off the coast of Maine. Rhoade, who knew the Maine coast well, joined the **FLYING HORSE** crew, but soon discovered that Aernouts continued to attack English and American vessels as well as French. Aernouts also attacked and defeated the French 30-man garrison at Castine, Maine, and built himself a fort at Machias, claiming the surrounding islands for Holland. In February of 1675, Captain Sam Mosley was hired by the Massachusetts General Court to track down and capture Aernouts and Rhoade. With the help of a French privateer, Mosley attacked the **FLYING HORSE** and the Dutch Fort at Machias, capturing many pirates. Back in Boston, Rhoade and the Dutch pirates were condemned to be hanged, but the war with local Indians, called *"King Philip's War,"* erupted — and the pirates were persuaded to join Mosley in fighting Indians.

Another pirate ship docked in Boston twelve years later. She was the ketch **SPARROW** from Barbadoes, Richard Narramore, a Bostonian, was the master. According to his testimony, he had been hired by 18 pirates, *"at a cost of forty pieces-of-eight apiece,"* to deliver them *"at different places"* along the East Coast, from New York to Newfoundland. These passengers, according to Narramore, were former pirates, returning home with their chests of treasures, to retire. The first pirate to be dropped off, *"landed at Gardner Island on Long Island, with two chests; a second went to Newport, Rhode Island; and two, with small chests, went to Damaras Cove."* Pirate John Danson and his treasure was brought to Boston, and Thomas Scudder, to Salem. Danson, Scudder, Christopher Goff of Rhode Island, Edward Calley and Thomas Dunston were arrested and brought before the Boston Magistrates. In Danson's treasure chest, which was confiscated, were 900 pieces-of-eight. He admitted that he had been a crewman, sailing with pirate Captain Henley, plundering Arab and Turkish merchant ships in the Red Sea. Like Danson, the other captives pleaded guilty to piracy, but since there was no one at Court to complain, or accuse them, they were released. *"Their money, silver plate and jewels given back to them,"* with, I'm sure, a hefty court fee paid out to the magistrates. Christopher Goff, with former Maine pirate Henry Halloway, were in fact, soon hired by the Massachusetts General Court to patrol the coast in search of other pirates. Cotton Mather's piety not withstanding, it seems that piracy and politics continued to mix well in New England.

Newport, Rhode Island, which Mather considered *"a den of thieves,"* was, without doubt, a haven for pirates. Such notables as Captain Kidd, Blackbeard, Tew, and Avery(Every) made it their port-of-call. Thomas Tew, as famous as Kidd in his day, was born and bred in Rhode Island. Two years after the **SPARROW** episode, in September 1688, a pirate named Peterson, with seventy men, *"in a bark of ten guns, came into Newport and refitted here,"* Towne Records reveal. A sea captain named Andrew Belcher paid for hides and elephant tusks that Peterson and his men had pirated off Africa, yet, *"a jury will not arrest him, for his crew is made up of neighbors."* The following year, when King William's War between France and England commenced, French privateersmen tried to attack and sack Block Island, but pirate Thomas Paine, who later became an associate of Captain Kidd's, sailed out of Newport and drove them off.

It wasn't too long thereafter that Governor Stoughton of Massachusetts wrote to the County Sheriff and to the Governor of Rhode Island the following: *"I am informed that sundry wicked and ill disposed persons are lately landed and set on shore on or about Long Island, Rhode Island, and parts adjacent, having brought with them quantities of foreign coins, silver, gold, bullion, merchandise and other treasure, some of which persons, unknown by name, may probably come into this Province and transport their moneys, merchandise and treasure hither. In his Majesty's name, I strictly command and require you to make diligent search within your several Precincts for such suspected persons."* Stoughton was constantly writing to friends in high places in England, complaining about Rhode Islanders *"who allow pirates in for a share of any prizes they bring into their port."* One of Stoughton's friends, wealthy London merchant Lewis Roberts, told Parliament that, *"much of Rhode Island currency is of pirate money."* William Clark, the noted marine historian of the 1700s, wrote that *"piracy was winked at in those days as part of the business of honest men... If a pirate was to get 1,000 pounds or two, he doubt not would find friends to get a pardon for him."*

Thomas Tew, Rhode Island's illustrious pirate, who the Royal Governor of New York, Thomas Fletcher, called *"a very pleasant man,"* sailed out of Newport and on to Bermuda in 1691. Unable to get a privateering commission at a reasonable fee from Rhode Island's Governor, who knew he was a pirate, Tew acquired one from the Governor of Bermuda to *"attack French vessels,"* which he never did. With his license to steal safely aboard his 70-ton sloop **AMITY**, he headed for the Red Sea and Indian Ocean to plunder Arabian and Indian vessels. In the spring of 1694, he was back in Newport with *"100,000 pounds sterling worth of elephant tusks of ivory, gold, silver, and jewels,"* and each of his sixty crew members *"with 1,200 pounds apiece,"* enough to allow them all to retire comfortably for the rest of their lives. Captain Tew, however, after depositing his treasure in and around Newport, most think at Sakonnet Point or Patience Island, he called for a new crew to return to the great island of Madagascar in the Indian Ocean, known as *"The Pirates' Kingdom."* To join the **AMITY** crew, *"servants ran from their masters and sons from their parents,"* said Rhode Island's Governor Cranston. Leaving Newport again, Tew stopped at New York City for his privateering commission, and to give Governor Fletcher a gold watch, his wife a fine necklace, and the Governor's daughters, gold and ruby rings. *"I like Thomas Tew,"* Governor Fletcher said, when asked why he befriended the pirate. *"I like hearing him talk."* For being too friendly with buccaneers, Governor Fletcher lost his job in 1698 and was recalled to England.

Governor Fletcher's bossom-buddy was Fred Philipse, a carpenter from Holland, who came to New York in 1647. By the time Tew started out on his second voyage, Philipse owned an estate covering 21 miles along the banks of the Hudson River and was considered the richest man in New York. His wealth was acquired by supplying vessels, foodstuffs, and other materials to the pirates of Madagascar. One of Philipse's *"kept"* pirates was Adam Baldridge, who was sent to set up a pirate tradingpost at St. Maries, a small island port off Madagascar. Part of Baldridge's shopping-list reads as follows: *"January 17, 1697 — Arrived **AMITY**, Captain Tew's Sloop, fitted into a brigantine by the owners of the **CHARMING MARY**, Captain Richard Glover, Commander. She was laden with several sorts of goods, part whereof I bought and part to Captain Hore* (a New York pirate commander). *. . . Feb. 13 — Arrived Capt. John Hore's prize from Persia, and Capt. Hore in the **JOHN & REBECKAH**., about 180-tons burden, 20 guns, 100 men. The prize about 300-ton, laden with calicoes. . . . Arrived **RESOLUTION**, Capt. Shivers, 200-tons, 90 men, 20 guns, formerly belonging to Capt. Glover, but the Company took her from him and 24 men, by reason they were not willing to go a privateering in the East Indies. While there, they took the **AMITY** for her water casks, sails, riggings and mast, for she met a monsoon at sea, and turned the hull adrift on a Reef. . . ."*

Although some of Tew's men were drowned when **AMITY** was all but smashed to splinters in the wild storm, Thomas Tew met his end in battle, boarding a prize ship of the Great Mogul of India, which was stuffed with gold, silver, and jewels. He was shot in the belly by an Indian soldier. As famous writer Daniel Defoe tells us, the gunshot *"carried away the rim of Tew's belly, who held his bowels with his hands for some small space."* Tew's crew, did manage to take the rich vessel, although she was defended by some 200 Indians, outnumbering the pirate crew three to one. After the monsoon, the remnants of Tew's crew joined the crew of the **FORTUNE**, Captain Thomas Mostyn, out of New York, a ship owned by Fred Philipse.

The **FORTUNE** sailed from Madagascar with the pirates and their treasure of the Great Mogul, in July of 1697. She arrived in New York about the same time as the new Royal Governor of New York and New England, the Earl of Bellomont, arrived there from England. Bellomont soon got word that the **FORTUNE** carried over one million dollars in treasure. He ordered the port-collector, Chidley Brooks, with a host of constables, to seize the ship and bring the treasure to him. Brooks refused, faining that the pirates would kill him if he tried. As Bellomont threatened to hang Brooks as a traitor, one of the constables alerted Captain Mostyn, and by the time Brooks and his men reluctantly boarded the **FORTUNE**, the real fortune in gold, silver and jewels, had been removed.

Bellomont got off a quick, angry letter to Parliament: *"When ships come into Boston and New York,"* he wrote, *"the Masters swear to their manifests, that is they swear to the number of parcels they bring, but the contents are unknown; then the merchants come and produce invoices, and whether true or false, is left to their ingenuity. . ."*

"The pirates have a fine harbour at Madagascar," Captain Thomas Warren of the **H.M.S WINDSOR** informed the King of England on November 28, 1697. *"They have built there a regular fort and mounted fifty guns. They have 1,500 men with seventeen ships and sloops, some mounted with forty guns. New York, New England, and the West Indies send them food and supplies. . ."*

"We amassed such a treasury at Madagascar," said Captain Henry Avery, *"as no society of men ever possessed. We had wealth enough not only to make us rich, but almost to have made a nation rich."* Avery, (also spelled Every,) was called *"King of the Pirates"* by Daniel Defoe. If acquired wealth through plundering was the measure to determine who was *"king"* of the pirates, then Avery beats out Captain Kidd, Blackbeard and all the others. After robbing many

Spanish and Portuguese vessels off Peru and in the West Indies, he and his 40-man crew opted to come to Madagascar and retire— but they got bored hanging around the island, so Avery and his crew sailed for Sumatra. *"It was there,"* he tells us in a Journal written years later, *"that I got news that two large ships belonging to the Great Mogul were expected to cross the bay from Hoogly, carrying his grand-daughter, who was to be married to the King of Pegu, with all her retinue, jewels and wealth. . . . There were three ships and our two vessels met them in the Bay of Bengal. The first ship, carrying guns, we attacked, and killed a great many of them* (Indian soldiers) *and made the rest run down under their hatches, crying out like creatures bewitched. We then chased the other ships. One was chiefly filled with women. The grand-daughter of the Great Mogul was our prize in the first ship. . .*

When my men had entered and mastered the ship, my lieutenant thought I alone should go into the great cabin, for the lady herself was there, and he feared the men were so heated they would murder her and her attendants, or do worse. . . . Such a sight of glory and misery was never seen by a buccaneer before. The queen was all in gold and silver, but frightened and crying. . . . She was in a manner covered with diamonds, and I soon let her see that I had more mind to the jewels than to the lady. . . I have heard that it has been reported in England that I ravished this lady, but they wrong me. . . We did indeed ravish them of all their wealth. . . ."

Avery let the Queen and all the other girls and Indian soldiers go, but took one of their ships, filled with the largest fortune ever pirated, back to Madagascar. *"I tell you the truth,"* he says, *"considering the costly things we took here, which we did not know the value of, and besides gold and silver and jewels, I say, we never knew how rich we were. . . . If we had been asked for a million of pieces-of-eight, or a million of pounds sterling, to have purchased our pardon, we should have been very ready to have complied with it, for we really knew not what to do with ourselves, or with our wealth. The only thing we had now before us was to consider what method to take for going home with our wealth, or at least with some part of it as would secure us easy and comfortable lives. . . ."*

Officially, Avery was never seen or heard from again. Rumor at the time was that he died, starved to death, trying to move his enormous treasure by camels through the deserts of either Persia or Africa. Others thought he had successfully escaped to France. When his Journal, titled *"A Long Tale of Piracy,"* was published in 1710, his whereabouts was unknown and he wanted to keep it that way. He admitted that he had buried much of his treasure, for he couldn't carry it all back to England, where it is assumed he ended up. He lamented in his Journal that, *"a little box full of invaluable jewels that the Queen had given to me, that I wish now were safe with me in England, for I doubt not but some of them are fit to be placed on the King's crown."*

On September 6, 1698, one of Avery's men, John Devin, was apprehended in Providence, Rhode Island. On September 20th, he went before the Magistrates, accused of piracy on the high seas. *"Devin,"* remarked Governor Bellomont, *"appears to be a sober man and reported wealthy."* Devin's testimony shocked Bellomont and the British Parliament, for it proved that Public Enemey Number One, Pirate Chief Henry Avery, had come to Rhode Island after leaving Madagascar, as did most of his cew. *"In April of 1696,"* said Devin, *"Capt. Every, alias Bridgemen, came into the Harbor of Providence with the ship CHARLES, alias FANCY, where the Captain and his ships crew, I being one of said Company, left behind the CHARLES and purchased other vessels to make their way to Ireland."* Devin said he did not know if others in the crew had remained in New England. He languished in jail for less than two months, but was then acquitted, for, after all, he was now a wealthy upstanding citizen of the community. He did, however, infer that the Governor of Rhode Island had helped Avery in purchasing the vessels and supplies needed to escape to the West Coast of Ireland. One of Avery's crew, with a heavy bag of gold and silver, was arrested in Galway. He testified that Avery had gone to Dublin, but Avery was never caught. Some Irish historians believe that Avery, alias Tom Bridgeman, lived out a long and comfortable life near Broadhaven on the West Coast of Ireland, where ex-pirates had always been welcomed. Another pirate chief, Captain Mainwaring, said of Broadhaven, *"It is a great spot for pyrates, for provisions and careening ships, and it has a good store of English, Scottish and Irish wenches, which resort unto them, and these are strong attractions to draw the common sort to them thither."*

Many pirates headquartered in Madagascar in 1697 headed for Broadhaven, Ireland and points in New York and New England, with their treasures. As Adam Baldridge, Fred Philipse's trader at the port of St. Maries, tells us, *"there was a Negro rising there, and the killing of whitemen. . . The men that were killed by the natives were most of them pirates that had been in the Red Sea and took several ships there. They were chiefly the occasion of the native Rising, by their abusing of the natives and taking of their cattle from them, and were most of them men that came from several ships as Capt. Rainor, Capt. Coats,*

Captain Hore and Capt. Stevens. . . . After good consideration, all my men and I agreed not to go back to St. Maries, but return to America. . ." It's interesting to note that, the famous Captain Kidd later told the Governor of Massachusetts that *"Adam Baldridge was the occasion for the native insurrection and the death of many pirates, for he inveigled a great many natives of St. Maries on his ship and sold them as slaves. The natives on the island revenged on those pirates by cutting their throats."* Whatever the cause, the result was a glut of pirates swarming into New York and New England, and the new Royal Governor of the Colonies was panic stricken.

"Since my leaving New York for Boston," Governor Bellomont wrote the Trade Lords of London, *"one of four ships has come in that went thence to Madagascar and of which has brought sixty pirates and a vast deal of treasure. I hear that every one of the pirates paid 150 £. for his passage, and the owners, I am told, have cleared thirty thousand pounds by this voyage. It is observable that Stephen Delancy, a hot-headed saucy Frenchman, and Mr. Hackshaw are the chief owners of this ship. I hear there were 200 pirates at Madagascar when the ship came away, who intended to take their passage in Frederick Phillip's* (Philipse's) *ship and the other two belonging to New York. A great ship has been seen off this Coast* (Boston, Massachusetts) *many times this week; it is supposed to be one Maise* (Mace), *a pirate, who has brought a vast deal of wealth from the Red Sea. There is a Sloop also at Rhode Island, which is said to be a pirate. We can do nothing towards the taking of those ships, for want of a Man-of-War."*

One pirate sloop that deposited pirates and treasure ashore in the dead of night at New York and Newport, Rhode Island, was the **NASSAU** from Madagascar. Captain Edward Coats was commander, who had previously paid Governor Fletcher 700 pounds in silver as protection money, but now, with Fletcher recalled to England in disgrace, he had to sneak into American ports to unload his cargo. A Colonel Baynard of New York appeared before the London Board of Trade in December of 1698, and said, *"pieces of Arabian gold, are common in New York and Rhode Island, after the arrival there of pyrate Captain Coats from the Red Sea."*

One Rhode Island pirate captain, whom Governor Bellomont was able to capture, was James Gillam, commander of the **MOCHA** frigate, once captained by Joshua Edgecomb. Gillam murdered Edgecomb, *"while the Captain was asleep,"* says Bellomont, *"and encouraged the ship's Company to turn pirates. Ever since, he has been robbing the Red Sea and Seas of India,"* he informed the Board of

Trade on November 29, 1699. *"Reports of men lately of Madagascar, say the MOCHA has taken above two million pounds sterling."* Bellomont, thrilled with his detective work in capturing Gillam, admitted, *"my taking of him was an accident. . . . On Saturday, October 11th, late in the evening, I got word that Gillam was in Rhode Island, but coming to Boston, so I had my Constables search all the Inns. At the first Inn they went to, they found Gillam's horse tied up in the yard, but he was not in the Inn. I offered 200 pieces-of-eight for information on him, and old pirate Captain Knot's wife said that Gillam had the alias of James Kelley, and was now in Charlestown. We seized Francis Dole of Charlestown, in whose house he was harbored, one of Hore's crew and one of Colonel Fletcher's pirates. We took Gillam behind Dole's house, womanizing. He is the most imprudent, hardened villain I ever saw. He has become a Mohammedan, and I had him searched by a Jew in this Towne, and he declared Gillam be circumsized. He is now in irons in the Gaol in Boston. . . . I am told that as Vice Admiral of these Provinces, I am entitled to one-third of Gillam's gold and jewels."*

Whether or not the industrious new Governor got a percentage of Gillam's gold and jewels is unknown, but 23 days later, he had the good fortune of capturing another pirate captain, William Sims, *"a man formerly burnt in the hand at Boston for stealing,"* says Bellomont. His ship, filled with East India goods valued at 27,000 pounds sterling, was seized off the Massachusetts coast. *"The cargo did come from Madagascar,"* Bellomont claimed, and Sims, *"who had gone forth a poor man and come back a Master and half owner of a ship,"* was placed in the Boston Gaol with Gillam. Bellomont, who paid dearly for information on pirates and the whereabouts of their treasures, was told by one of his active spies that both Sims and Gillam had anchored off Block Island and Gardner Island before they were captured, *"and were visited by John Gardner, the Deputy Collector of Rhode Island,"* before they sailed away. He is the same Gardner who owned Gardner's Island off Rhode Island and near Long Island, where much of Captain Kidd's treasure was uncovered two years later. In November, 1699, Bellomont informed the Board of Trade in England that, *"Gardner is accused to have been a pirate. I doubt he will foreswear himself rather than part with Gillam's gold."*

Another frequenter of Block Island and Gardner Island off Rhode Island, was Captain Joe Brodish, a Cambridge lad, who started his notorious career while serving as boatswain aboard the ADVENTURE. This 350-ton, 22-gun merchant ship arrived off the coast of

Connecticut on March 18th, 1699. At this time, Brodish was her commander, having killed the **ADVENTURE**'s original and lawful captain, Thomas Gulleck. Then Brodish led the crew in a series of pirate ventures in the Caribbean. He returned to New England and attempted to deposit nine chests of Spanish coins and jewelry for safe keeping at John Gardner's *"Pirate Bank,"* but a storm kept the **ADVENTURE** crew from landing. Instead, Brodish sailed into Newport and sent two of his men ashore in a rowboat to buy a sloop, so that some of the crew might sail on to Maine and bury their treasures there. Unfortunately, the two crewmen were arrested and thrown in jail. Undaunted, Brodish stopped a passing sloop while he lay at anchor, and bought her with silver bars from a surprised but agreeable Newport fisherman. Some of the treasure was transfered from the **ADVENTURE** to the fishing sloop, and then both vessels sailed for Montauk Point. Some of Brodish's crew, who were captured later, said the **ADVENTURE** was purposely scuttled off Montauk, Rhode Island, and Brodish with his crew sailed on to Maine. Legend is that the **ADVENTURE** began sinking in a raging sea and finally went under, with over two million dollars in treasure going down with her, and that Brodish and the crew swam ashore. Whichever the case, Brodish himself, with his one-eyed sidekick, Tee Wetherly, came into Boston in April, was recognized and the two were arrested. Nine other members of the **ADVENTURE** crew were eventually rounded up in Rhode Island and Massachusetts. In their possession was about *"3,000 pounds sterling."* Every crew member aboard the **ADVENTURE**, it was reported, *"received 1,500 pieces-of-eight before he left the ship. Some 3,000 pounds with jewels belonging to Brodish were seized by authorities at the home of Henry Pierson, Nassau Island, New York."* Brodish and Wetherly languished in Boston Gaol for two months, but on June 25th, the jail keeper reported that the two had escaped. Governor Bellomont was furious. *"About a fortnight ago,"* he wrote the Board of Trade, *"Brodish and another pirate got out of the Gaol of this Towne and escaped, with the consent of the Gaoler Mr. Ray, as there is a great reason to believe."* — Caleb Ray, the jail keep, was Joe Brodish's cousin.

Bellomont offered a reward of 200 pieces-of-eight for the capture of Brodish, and 100 pieces of silver for Tee Wetherly. One bounty hunter who took up the challenge to track them down was an Abenaki Indian chief named Essacambuit. He caught up with the escapees in Saco, Maine, which might lead one to believe that their treasures were hidden near there. The Sachem-sleuth offered the pirates death or a peaceful journey to Boston. Back in jail, the pirates attempted two more escapes, but were caught before they made it out of Boston. Bellomont fired Brodish's cousin Caleb. *"I believe the new gaoler I have got is honest,"* said Bellomont, *"otherwise I should be very uneasy."* Just to be on the safe side, he had Brodish and Wetherly shipped off to England, where they were tried for piracy and hanged.

The death of Brodish was not the end of pirate activity in Rhode Island— only the beginning of the end. The eighteenth century started out with a bumper crop of Rhode Island pirates, and in 1702, so William Clark the maritime historian reveals, *"every man of Newport was a privateersman or a pirate."* In 1716, Edward Teach, better known as Blackbeard, paid a long visit to Providence, and three years later, Captain Ben Norton *"sailed out of Providence in a brigantine to the West Indies,"* writes John Menzies, then New England's Royal Secretary of the Admiralty, *"Norton's vessel by common observation, is more fit for pirates than trade."* Norton joined notorious pirate chief Thomas *"Black Bart"* Roberts in the West Indies, and in tandem, they took a Spanish treasure ship *"and a Dutch ship of 250-tons, loaded with a cargo of considerable value."* A few months later, Admiral Menzies' writes, *"Norton came with his ship and cargo into Tarpaulin Cove at the Elizabeth Islands; where pirates used to come to infest the coast; and he did, in a clandestine manner, advise Joseph Whipple of his arrival."* Whipple was the owner of Norton's ship, who later became Deputy Governor of Rhode Island. *"Whipple and Norton,"* writes Admiral Menzies, *"carried off the rich cargo, with other traders of Newport, in sloops to Providence. . . Yet, when I went to the Governor of Rhode Island, he would not give up the goods."* So it seems, the passage of time from one century to the next, did not change the times that politicians dirtied their hands in Rhode Island. Although piracy was tempered somewhat in other New England ports, Providence and Newport remained havens for cocky pirates and crooked politicians. This freeport for freebooters was rudely awakened in 1723, however, when at Gravelly Point near Newport, twenty-six men were hanged for *"piracy,"* — this definitely took the wind out of alot of Rhode Island pirate sails.

III
THE MARBLE BOYS OF MARBLEHEAD

In Lynn, Massachusetts, once the shoemaking capitol of America, the citizens were recently up in arms. The state wanted to build a super highway through the Lynn Woods to hook up with an inter-state highway system. The residents won their battle and the road was stopped.

Lynn doesn't have many wooded sections today and what little remains the people are determined to save. Also, the first shoemaker of Lynn, a reformed pirate, once lived in the woods at a place called Dungeon Rock. Two men from nearby Marblehead, Massachusetts spent their entire lives searching for treasure there in the 19th century. Hiram Marble tunneled through Dungeon Rock from the late 1840's to November 1868, and his son Edwin continued digging the man-made cave in Lynn Woods until 1880, when he died. Neither, as far as we know, found a trace of treasure. Hiram claimed that a fortune teller had told him that treasure was buried at Dungeon Rock and that he would find it. An old Lynn legend adds some credence to the prophesy:

A pirate ship sailed into the Saugus River bordering the woods in 1657 and dropped anchor. Four seamen rowed away from the ship and continued up the river as the ship set sail again and returned to sea, never to be seen again. Besides a few houses, there was an iron foundry located on the river bank. It is now known as the Saugus Ironworks, built in 1642, birthplace of America's iron and steel industry. A few days after the pirate ship had departed, a note was left at the iron foundry door from the four pirates who had rowed up the river into the woods. The note read that these men wanted hatchets and shackles made and that if the forge foreman agreed to make the articles and leave them at the edge of the woods, they would provide him *poundage of silver.* The foreman, however, was to keep their request secret as part of the bargain, but he boasted to his friends about the handsome reward he received for his work.

Word of a pirate band living in the Lynn Woods spread, and soon a British man-o-war sailed up the river, and armed Redcoats entered the woods to capture the pirates. Three of the four were caught napping in a valley some two miles into the woods, where they had built a hut and had planted a garden. The place today is known as *Pirate's Glenn.* They were brought aboard the man-o-war, shipped back to England, and hanged. The fourth pirate, Thomas Veal, escaped the British by retreating deep into the woods and hiding in a cave which is now known as

Dungeon Rock. Pirate Veal made the cave his home, and there he crafted shoes from animal leather which he traded for food and utensils with neighboring Lynn villagers. Rumors spread that Veal was harboring a treasure in the cave, but no one discovered the truth of this speculation, for in the summer of 1658, New England experienced a violent earthquake which blocked the entrance to the cave with large boulders, shutting Pirate Veal inside, where he supposedly perished.

Records of Thomas Veal as a pirate are scarce, but he did sail his ketch with 14 pirate crewmen aboard into New London, Connecticut to buy cannons, but this was in the summer of 1685. *"Graham and Veale have silver plate and their crew ware plush clothing,"* the Governor of Connecticut revealed to the Massachusetts Legislature. A merchant sea captain, John Prentice, went directly to the Massachusetts General Court about the same time to complain directly that, *"a sloop of Captain Veale, with Harvey, a merchant, on board did chase my vessel, shooting cannons, off Cape Anne,"* but Prentice was saved when Veale's vessel was driven away in a storm. The Massachusetts Governor also was informed that *"Veale committed piracy in Virginia."* He sent out an armed brig in pursuit, *"Richard Patteshall in command, with Captain Sampson Waters,"* but they couldn't find Veal and his men. Maybe that was when Veal slipped into the Saugus River, buried his treasure in the Lynn cave and remained in the Lynn Woods. Thomas Veal, also spelled *"Veale and Vealey"* in old records, was born and brought up in Lynn, but was unlawfully active in 1685, according to the records, and not in 1658 as the old legend indicates. Essex County court records show that on June 21, 1685, *"Thomas Vealey of Lynn, is accussed of theft of pewter from the Salem home of Captain Gershome Browne."* He is to *"pay treble damages or be whipped twenty stripes."* Tom took the lashes and, apparently, that is when he decided to become a pirate instead of a house robber, in 1685 and not 1658.

A Lynn spiritualist, supposedly talking directly to Pirate Veal, passed on information to Hiram Marble, or possibly to Hiram's father, as to the exact whereabouts of the treasure at Dungeon Rock. Hiram bought the land surrounding and including Dungeon Rock in 1852, where he had already begun a deep excavation to find Pirate Veal's body and his treasure. Prior to this, in 1834, other treasure hunters *"placed a keg of powder in the cave,"* writes Lynn's 19th century historian Alanzo Lewis, *"which on its explosion blew out the lower portion of the rock, causing a large mass above to fall, and thus destroying the cavern..."* Hiram used sledges, crowbars, and explosives to chip and blow away the hard rock, but by 1862 he had tunneled only 135 feet.

Hiram had chiseled out stairs into his hand-made cave, which measured seven feet high by six feet wide. At about that time, Hiram moved from Marblehead and built a house in the Lynn Woods to be near his work. When Hiram's son, Edwin, was old enough, he helped his father by carrying buckets of chipped rock out of the cave. Today, a pile of rock chips over 200 feet high and 40 feet wide is located near the cave entrance. When Hiram died on November 10, 1868, probably from his strenuous labor inside the damp cave, Edwin continued to tunnel through the rock for twelve more years. The Marbles spent all their savings and a total of 22 years on the project, but always expected that at the next crack of the hammer or pick, they would break through into Pirate Veal's sealed tomb. Anyone who ventured into the Lynn Woods, day or night, would hear the continuous tapping, and conclude it was the ghost of Pirate Veal still making shoes when, in reality, it was Edwin Marble striking his sledge-hammer against the rocks. Edwin died in 1880, but the 200-foot man-made cave remains in Lynn Woods at Dungeon Rock as a monument to his and his father's life work at unsuccessful treasure hunting.

Today, a rusty iron gate blocks off the cave to trespassers, for there are many who still believe that by digging a few more feet, they might break into Veal's cave and find his treasure. The Marble Cave is eerie and usually filled with knee-deep water in the Spring. Friends of mine who grew up in Lynn, say that they would sometimes visit the cave in their youth, usually at Dusk. Inevitably they would flee the place in panic when they heard that ever-present tapping from within the cave— the ghosts of the Marbles, still at work in the treasure cave at Dungeon Rock.

Hiram Marble stands at entrance to cave at Dungeon Rock, where Pirate Veale (right) hid his treasure. Photo, and sketch by C.A. Lawrence, courtesy of the Lynn Historical Society.

IV
HERE'S LOOKING AT YOU, KIDD

According to books, newspaper articles, magazine features, and local legends, famous pirate captain William Kidd buried his treasure in hundreds of spots throughout the World. The most popular designated locations for his hidden loot, however, seem to be in New England. People have been searching for it for almost three centuries, and a bit of it has been found. The first to dig up some of Kidd's buried gold, silver and jewels was Richard Coote, alias Lord Bellomont, Governor of New York, Massachusetts and New Hampshire. At Gardner's Island, off the eastern end of Long Island, New York, with the help of the Massachusetts militia, he uncovered 91 pounds and 8 ounces of gold bars and gold dust, 196 pounds of silver bars and coins, and two pounds of diamonds and other precious stones — but this was back in 1699. Another hefty portion of Kidd's loot was uncovered at Conanicut Island, now Jamestown, Rhode Island, in 1891. It was found by workmen digging a cellar-hole under the summer house of Seth Vose. The 17th century home was once owned by a pirate named Tom Payne, who was one of Kidd's mates. According to Bob Vose, Seth's grandson, (owner of Vose Galleries, Newbury Street, Boston), *"a quantity of elephant tusks, silver coins and gold doubloons were found buried deep under the house by two workmen."* Bob Vose, who lives in Duxbury, Massachusetts today, goes on to say that, *"I was told by my grandfather that one of the men digging the cellar, soon after finding the treasure, and supposedly turning over what he found, left my grandfather's employ, moved to New Hampshire, bought two houses, and retired from the life of hard labor."*

Charles Sanderson of Kingston, Massachusetts, a successful treasure hunter, who recently uncovered the archaeological riches of the Revolutionary War wreck **GENERAL ARNOLD** in the mudflats of Plymouth Harbor, told me that he had uncovered new evidence indicating that Kidd's long lost treasure is buried under Logan Airport in Boston, Massachusetts. Sanderson informed me that Kidd's great-great-great grandson had discovered an old jar in the attic of his Connecticut home. The jar contained a coded map which located a small island in Boston Harbor, now covered with tarmack, as the spot where Kidd buried his treasure before sailing into Boston, where he was arrested and jailed by Lord Bellomont. Other treasure hunters believe that Kidd buried his treasure at nearby Deer Island, now part of Winthrop, where many silver coins were found by workmen building a seawall there in the earlier part of this century. Because of the Deer Island Jail, treasure hunters do not have access to the island. Given permission to search the outer peninsula of the island by the Suffolk County Sheriff in 1984, eight expert *"shooters,"* or metal-detecting enthusiasts and myself, scoured the island near the seawall at Deer Island for a day, but we came up empty handed.

Deer Island, Maine is another presumed location of Kidd's buried loot. Supposedly, as William Kidd was escorted under guard to the gallows in England, he whispered a series of numbers to his devoted wife, but the numbers, *"44106818,"* always remained a mystery to her. In 1894, noted astronomer David Todd, of Amherst College, revealed the meaning of the number code as the latitudinal and longitudinal coordinates of Deer Island, Maine. These are 44 degrees 10' by 68 degrees 13', very similar to the numbers presented to Mrs. Kidd by her condemned husband.

Deer Island had been owned by the Olmstead family of Maine since 1696. It had been given as a gift by the Penobscot Indian chief to Cotton Mather Olmstead that year, after Cotton successfully treated the chief's wounds when he was mauled by a bear. In 1894, after Professor Todd revealed his solution to Captain Kidd's number-code, Marion Olmstead made an intensive search of the island for the treasure and found a hidden cave at the waters edge that flooded twice a day at high tide. *"Inside the cave on its sandy floor,"* reported Marion to her father Fred Olmstead, who owned the island, *"was a rectangular hole in the clay, about fifteen by thirty inches on the surface and about fifteen inches deep. The bottom of the hole and sides, were heavily coated with iron rust — an iron box apparently had been removed. As there were various legends relative to the presence of Captain Kidd upon the Maine Coast, the discovery of the excavation was sufficient to awaken eager interest in the question of the iron box and the person who carried it away."*

After researching old family journals and diaries, Fred and Marion discovered that, in 1801, a Canadian named Jacques Cartier had tried to buy Deer Island from their ancestor, Oliver Olmstead, but he refused to sell. Cartier rented a portion of the island from Olmstead instead, and built himself a cabin. He remained on the island only a few months however, and then disappeared, never to been seen or heard from again by Oliver Olmstead. Oliver recorded that he visited Cartier's abandoned cabin one day and found part of a letter on the cabin floor, which read: *". . . Absolute secrecy must be observed. . .(* signed) *John Jacob Astor."* Oliver Olmstead thought nothing more of the strange note signed by Astor to Cartier, but Oliver's descendants did. They were aware that John Jacob Astor was considered one of the richest men in the world by

1805. Fred Olmstead researched further in New York City and discovered that Cartier had worked for Astor prior to 1801, and that in 1802, Astor had presented Cartier with a check for $5,000 for *"meritorious service."* Fred Olmstead believed the *"meritorious service"* was the digging up of the treasure chest from the cave, now called *"Captain Kidd's Cave,"* located on his Deer Island property. Olmstead believed it was the treasure in this chest that made John Jacob Astor a multimillionaire. Although John Jacob Astor was long since dead in 1896, Fred Olmstead sued the entire Astor family who had inherited their father's fortune. Olmstead figured the Astors owed him $5,112,235.50. How he came to this figure, nobody, but Fred Olmstead, knew.

The court case, so Fred Olmstead periodically reported in the newspapers, was still in litigation 23 years later, but on April 1st, 1922, the entire truth of the matter was revealed by Olmstead: *"It is all a hoax,"* he reported in the Worcester Massachusetts Telegram, *"an April Fools Day joke that blossomed over the years... This interesting and amazing yarn has been in circulation since 1894,"* he reported, *"when it was written for the amusement of myself and my daughter. Unfortunately, in passing from hand to hand and especially from mouth to mouth, it has often lost its delightful humorous quality, but because of the endless chain of inquiries from friends, acquaintances and total strangers, I thought it must end here — F.L. Olmstead."* And so, the quest for Captain Kidd's treasure at Deer Island, Maine came to an end. One wonders however, if the numerical code passed on to Mrs. Kidd from her husband was part of the hoax or indeed a reality, for it is known that Kidd desperately wanted to pass information on to her about his hidden treasure. In England, she was refused visitations with him while he languished in jail.

That Kidd left untold riches buried in the ground can not be denied. Eleven days before he died, while waiting execution in Newgate Prison May 12, 1701, he wrote his final pleading letter to Robert Harley, British parliamentarian, which read: *"In my late proceedings in the Indies I have lodged goods and treasure to the value of one hundred pounds, which I desire the Government may have the benefit of, in order thereto I shall desire no manner of liberty but to be kept prisoner on board such ship as may be appointed for that purpose, and only give the necessary directions, and in case I fail therein, I desire no favor but to be forthwith executed according to my sentence. If your honorable house will please to come to me, I doubt not to give such satisfaction as may obtain mercy, Your unfortunate humble servant, William Kidd."* Parliament, and the Magistrates refused Kidd's request to dig up his own treasure, and so, unless someone has secretly dug it up since, the loot that Kidd *"lodged"* somewhere, remains in its hiding place.

Some believe the famous *"money pit"* at Oak Island, Mahone Bay, Nova Scotia that has been dug into unsuccessfully since the mid-eighteenth century is where Captain Kidd hid his fortune. Others are convinced his treasure is *"in the fissures of large rock formations, inaccessible at high tide,"* located on Thimble and Money Islands, Stony Creek, Connecticut. Many have dug for Kidd's treasure at Chebeague Island, Casco Bay, Maine, and at nearby Jewell Island. A Mr. Chase who lived on Jewell Island supposedly found some of it using a map that Captain Kidd's black servant had drawn out and given to him. Block Island, off Rhode Island, is also a favorite spot for the hunters of Kidd's treasure. There is concrete evidence that Kidd stopped at Block Island, as he had at Gardiner's Island, before he was confined to Boston Jail. The list of island locations up and down the New England Coast where Kidd supposedly buried his treasure seems endless. There is even a *"Captain Kidd's - Island"* near Turner's Falls, Massachusetts, far inland and close to the Vermont border, where locals swear Captain Kidd hid his treasure. *"After all,"* they will tell you, *"how do you think the island got its name?"*

Richard Knight of Briton, England and Fred Graham of Belmont, California went looking for Kidd's treasure off the coast of Vietnam in June of 1983. Knight told officials that he had a map, *"gotten from my grandfather, showing an island off Vietnam where Kidd hid his treasure."* The young men went to the island of Phu Quoc, Vietnam and disappeared— believed to have been taken prisoners by the Viet-Cong. Captain Kidd's treasure fever is worldwide and as obsessive to treasure hunters today as it was back in the eighteenth and nineteenth centuries.

Besides the unanswered question of where Kidd hid his treasure is the question that will never be satisfactorily answered— why William Kidd went into piracy in the first place. He, of course, denied to his dying day that he was a pirate. Although tried for piracy, he was never convicted of it— yet, there is no question today that he was a pirate, and the most famous of the lot. Before going astray he was a wealthy, happily married gentleman, living in the high society of New York City. *"Others made me the tool of their avarice and ambition,"* Kidd said in an attempt to explain his unlawful actions. *"I was partly cajol'd and partly menaced into it,"* he told Robert Harley, *"by Lord Bellomont and one Robert Livingstone of New York."* Some historians believe that Kidd, the wealthy merchant, became a privateersman in middle-age because he had knowledge of a hidden treasure buried on an island in the Indian

Ocean, but there is no evidence of this.

William Kidd was born at Dundee, Scotland in 1654. As a youth, he became a merchant seaman, sailing to Nova Scotia and New England. By age 25, he was a successful merchantman skipper trading in the West Indies out of Boston and New York. In 1689, he commanded a privateer against the French in the West Indies, mentioned in various British dispatches from Captain Hewetson, for leading successful raids on St. Martins and Marie Galantee, but his crew mutinied after these raids, dropping him off on a deserted beach and sailing off as pirates to Nova Scotia. Two years later, June 8, 1691, Kidd was in Boston, hired by Massachusetts to hunt down Nova Scotian pirates, many of them his old crewmembers. The letter of negotiation reads: *"for Captain Kidd to go forth in His Majesty's service, to suppress an enemy privateer now upon these coasts."* Kidd was also involved in Governor William Phipps' expedition out of Boston the following year, against the French and Indians in Canada. Coincidentally, the vessel he commanded in that Acadian venture was the **ADVENTURE**, the same name as the galley he commanded three years later during his famous pirating venture. There is record in Boston of Captain Kidd bringing in a French vessel he captured in Maine waters, on August 17, 1691, *"to receive one-tenth of the prize money upon sale of the ship."*

Kidd married the wealthy widow, Sarah Bradley Cox Oort, of New York City, on May 16, 1691, the day after her husband John Oort died. Oort was Kidd's second mate aboard the **ADVENTURE**. Sarah lived in a mansion at 56 Wall Street, and she and her brother owned most of the property on the street, but Kidd built her a new brick mansion in downtown Manhattan, and that's where Sarah bore William two daughters, Sarah and Elizabeth. A friend and neighbor to them was Robert Livingstone, a fellow Scot who also married into money. It was Livingstone who was friendly with Richard Coote, the British Earl of Bellomont, convincing the Earl and Kidd that chasing after pirates and their treasures might be a lucrative business. Official pirate-hunting seemed even more enticing once Coote was appointed Governor of New York, Massachusetts and New Hampshire by the King in 1695. That year, Kidd and Livingstone sailed for London to see Coote before he officially took office in America. There Livingstone convinced the new Governor that, *"Kidd is a bold and honest man, the most fit in the Colonies to go against these wicked and ill-disposed persons who commit many and great Pyracies, Robberies, and Depredations upon the seas."* Livingstone made it plain that most of these pirates came from New England and New York, and would be recognized on sight by Kidd. Coote then persuaded King William to *"give and grant full power and authority to Captain William Kidd, as Commander of the ship ADVENTURE GALLEY, to seize and take pyrates Thomas Tews, John Ireland, Thomas Wake, William Mace, and all other pyrates and free-booters into custody."* The King, however, wisely did not offer a vessel from the British Navy, but suggested that the Earl of Bellomont supply the ship for Kidd's venture. Bellomont organized a private syndicate involving: the Earl of Orford, who was First Lord of the Admiralty, Sir John Somers, who was Chancellor and Lord Keeper of the Great Seal, the Duke of Shewsbury, who was also England's Secretary of State, and the Earl of Romney, England's Master General of Ordinance. Between them, they raised 6,000 pounds sterling to purchase and fit out the **ADVENTURE GALLEY**. Kidd and Livingstone were required to put up 20% of the needed venture capital, and the King insisted on 10% of any treasure profits. Kidd received his letter-of-marque for privateering on December 11, 1695. His commission was not just for apprehending notorious pirates, but to capture enemy vessels as well, French vessels in particular. Bellomont and his royal friends of the syndicate were to get 75% of all profits after the King and the crew got their shares, and Kidd and Livingstone were to receive 25% of the net profits. If no treasures or prize money was forthcoming, the crew would receive nothing for their labors, and Livingstone would have to pay back Bellomont for all expenses incured. Bellomont had Livingstone give him security bonds as collateral.

Kidd was pleased with the seaworthiness of the 287-ton, 34-gun **ADVENTURE GALLEY**, convinced that she was bigger and faster than any vessel a pirate chief might have under his command. He was also satisfied with the business deal, *"I thinking myself safe,"* he later commented, *"with a King's commission and the protection of so many great men."* He sailed from England bound for New York, with 70 English crewmen aboard, on April 23, 1696. Scrounging up more crew members in New York and Rhode Island, many of them being known pirates, he sailed out of New York for Maderas on September 6 th with a crew of 150 men. *"I thence sailed for the Cape of Good Hope,"* Kidd records, *"and on the 12th of December 1696, met four English Men of War; and I sailed a week in their company. I then parted and sailed to Telere, Madagascar. There, on or about the 29th of January, came a sloop belonging to Barbados, loaded with rum, sugar, powder and shot, with a French master, a Mr. Holton. He came on board our Galley and was suddenly taken ill there, and died in the cabin."* A few of the **ADVENTURE** crewmen, later present at Kidd's trial, hinted that Kidd had killed Mr. Holton but there was no evidence of this. Kidd took the sloop as a prize, *"it keeping us company,"* until the **ADVEN-TURE** arrived at the island of Mehila, near the pirate haven of Johanna, *"where we careened the Galley, and about fifty men died there of fever in a week's time,"* Kidd reported. *"On the 25th day of April, 1697, set sail for India, and came upon the coast of Mallabar in September, and went into Carrwarr to water...*

Afterwards, I continued upon the coast, cruising upon the Cape of Comorin, south of Hindustan, for Pirates that frequent that Coast, til November, when we met with Captain How in the **LOYAL CAP-TAIN,** *an English ship, whom I examined, and finding his Pass good, designed freely to let her pass about her affairs, but having two Dutch-men aboard, they told my men that there were Greeks and Armenians on board who had precious stones and other rich goods, which caused my men to be mutinous and got up their arms. They swore they would take the ship, and two-thirds of my men voted the same. I told them that I had come not to take any Englishmen or lawful traders, and that if they attempted any such thing they should never come aboard this Galley again, for I had no commission to take any but the King's enemies and pirates. I could scarce restrain them from their unlawful design, but at last prevailed."*

Some of Kidd's crewmen, who later testified against him at his trial in England, disagreed with Kidd's reported actions concerning Captain How's ship. A crewman, Benjamin Franks, said that, *"Kidd chased and plundered a small ship under English colors. The people of the ship were tortured to make them confess where their money was... I, at Carrwarr, and eight more, finding ourselves to be on board a pirate ship, made our escape from the* **ADVENTURE GALLEY.**" Another crewman, James How, testified that, *"Kidd murdered several English, and Dutch among 'em, of the* **LOYAL CAPTAIN,** *and all the Arabs* (Greeks and Armenians). *He got the commander aboard as a prisoner and took out of the English ship, one-hundred pieces of gold and precious stones."* At his trial, Kidd said that, *"all of which I testify to, Captain How will attest to, if living,"* but, of course, if Kidd killed Captain How, then the captain couldn't verify his statements. **ADVENTURE** crewman Darby Mullins testified that everything Kidd said about the **LOYAL CAPTAIN** was true, but Darby, an Irishman who was *"miraculously preserved from the great earthquake at Port Royal, Jamaica,"* was a known pirate. He was hanged with Captain Kidd, and for some unknown reason, James How, *"a sensible man who was pardoned,"* the court records reveal, gave the Keeper of Newgate Prison 300 pieces-of-eight to let him out of jail two months early. He returned to his home in Pennsylvania, where, as one old historian reports, *"he made considerable discoveries in the woods there."* After Kidd's trial, five other members of his crew that were pardoned after testifying against him, returned to the Americas. One to New York, one to Barbadoes, and three to New England.

According to Captain Kidd, *"My Journal was violently taken from me in the Port of St. Marie's in Madagascar"* (by the majority of his crew), and therefore, we must rely on his court testimony in England and his pretrial written statements in Boston, when he was obviously glossing over a few incidents to save his neck. The incident that finally sent him to the gallows, not for piracy but for murder, occured soon after the **LOYAL CAPTAIN** episode, when Kidd says, *"I refused to attack a Dutch ship, which infuriated my crew."* During this near-mutiny, Kidd reports that he called the leader of this insurrection, a gunner named William Moore, *"a lousy dog."* Moore replied, according to Kidd, *"if I am a lousy dog, then you have made me so. You have brought me to ruin."* Kidd then *"took a wooden bucket bound with iron hoops and struck Moore on the right side of the head, of which he died next day."* Kidd is insinuating that Moore mutinied because the Captain wouldn't turn pirate, upset that the **ADVENTURE** had been to sea for almost a year without taking a valuable prize. Some of the crewmen who testified however, said that Moore told Kidd that, *"you have ruined us all,"* meaning that Kidd had driven them into piracy, and if caught, they would be hanged as pirates. Crewmembers reported that before Kidd broke Moore's skull with the bucket, *"several ships had been taken, one prize being landed at Malabar Island, where Kidd shot a native, and burned and pillaged several villages."*

If we are to believe Kidd's narrative, he reports that, *"on November 19, I met with a Moore's ship, 200-tons, coming from Suratt, bound for Mallabar, having about forty Moors on board. On February 1st, 1698, upon the same coast, under French colors, with a design to decoy, I met with a Bengal Merchantman of Surat, 500-tons, ten guns, with French Passes. These two prizes I took to St. Maries, my Galley leaking so badly that I feared she would have sunk every hour. On the first day of April, 1698, I came into St. Maries in Madagascar. On the 6th of May, the lesser prize was hauled into the careening Key, the other not being arrived, and was ransacked and sunk by the mutinous men, who threatened me and the men who would not join with them, to burn and sink the other, that we might not go home and tell the news."*

"When I arrived in port," Kidd continues, *"there was a pyrate ship called the MOCA FRIGATE at anchor, Robert Culliford com-*

*mander, who, with his men, left the ship at my coming in, and ran into
the woods, but 97 of my men then deserted me and went to the MOCA,
and sent into the woods for the pyrates and brought Culliford and his
men on board again. Said deserters, sometimes in great numbers,
came on board our prize, which was the QUEDAH MERCHANT,
and carried away great guns, powder, shot, and what else they pleased, and threatened several times to murder me. After they had plundered and ransacked sufficiently, they went inland four miles to Edward
Welch's house."* (Welch was a New Englander, who had come to
Madagascar many years before, and his house was a fort.) *"At Welch's
house,"* Kidd reports, *"where my chest was lodged, they broke it open
and took out ten ounces of gold, forty pounds of plate, 370 pieces-of-
eight, my Journal, and a great many papers that belonged to me. . .
About June 15, the MOCA FRIGATE went away, manned by 130
men and forty guns, as pyrates. I was left with 13 men. The AD-
VENTURE GALLEY would not stay above water and she sank in
the Harbour. I, with my men, went on board the QUEDAH
MERCHANT, where we were forced to stay five months for a fair
wind. In the meantime some passengers presented, that were bound
for these parts, which I took on board to help to bring the prize
QUEDAH MERCHANT home."*

One wonders, is this where the phrase, *"He's got to be kidding,"*
comes from? Here's a Captain, hired to hunt down pirates, and he
brings his disabled vessel into the biggest pirate nest in the world, and
sends two prize ships loaded with treasure in there too — and he does
this with a crew that, so he says, has near-mutinied twice, and is
peppered with men that Kidd must have known were involved in piracy
in the past. What was his treasure chest doing at Welch's house? Welch
was a well known pirate. Kidd indicates that the QUEDAH MER-
CHANT was under a French Pass, supposedly captained by a Frenchman, under contract to the Great Mogul of Bengal. The few members of
Kidd's crew who were captured to stand trial with him in England testified, except for Darby Mullins, that the master of the QUEDAH
MERCHANT was an Englishman named Wright, and that she carried
over half a million pounds sterling worth of ivory, gold, gold dust, silver
and jewels. Two of the crew said that Kidd didn't chase the captain and
crew of the MOCA FRIGATE away when he entered St. Maries
Harbor, but *"drank with these pyrates from a tub of Bamboo on deck,
mixed with water, lime and sugar."* It seems that Kidd and notorious
pirate Robert Culliford were old friends. Kidd's statement that he was
"forced" to stay five months on the island, waiting for a fair wind to return
to America, also sounds a little ridiculous — no seaman waits five

months for a fair wind. The other prize Moore's ship, her name never revealed, was *"ransacked and sunk by the mutinous crew, "* Kidd says, but otherwise, little is mentioned of her, and one wonders why. Rear Admiral Benbow, cruising the West Indies in 1699, ran into one of Kidd's old crewmen, who told him that his captain had *"murdered all forty Moors aboard that vessel. "* Again one wonders why Kidd would commit such a crime, if not to keep the ship's contents secret. As the old pirate saying goes, *"dead men tell no tales. "*

Kidd, with his 13 man crew and *"passengers, "* who were probably pirates of Madagascar returning home with their ill-gotten booty, reported that the **QUEDAH MERCHANT** *"arrived at AnGuilla in the West Indies about the beginning of April 1699, and I sent my boat on shore. Here my men had the news that I and my people were proclaimed pirates, which incensed my people more and more. "* The Council President of the Leeward Islands, wrote to the British Board of Trade that, *"Kidd came here from Mallagascoe in a large vessel of 400-tons, thirty guns and eighty men, and his men mutinied, and 30 lost their lives. His vessel is very leaky and they are very much in want of provisions. Several of his men have deserted him, so he has not above 25 or 30 hands. He sailed for the island of St. Thomas and anchored there for three days, but the Governor denied him and he bore away. We forthwith have ordered the ship* **QUEENEBURROGH** *to make its way after him. "*

The British Board of Trade, upon the request of England's East India Company, who monopolized trade in India and the Orient, informed all British Crown Colonies throughout the world that *"Captain William Kidd is an obnoxious pyrate, and we urge his capture. "* Even though a *"General Pardon to all pyrates who surrender, "* was issued by the King of England in December of 1698, two exceptions were made to this lenient offer, *"Captain William Kidd and Captain Henry Avery are excluded. "*

Although Kidd himself made no reference to another mutiny of his most dedicated crewmen in the West Indies, he reports, *"I left St. Thomas and set sail for Moona, an island between Hispaniola and Puerto Rico, where we met with a sloop called the* **SAINT ANTHONY**, *bound for Montego from Curaso, Mr. William Bolton, merchant and Samuel Ward, Master. "* It is interesting to note, that William Bolton was an alias, the merchant owner of the **SAINT ANTHONY** was Abraham Redwood, who lived on the island of Antigua and, like the Mullins family, picked up stakes after Kidd was captured and moved to settle permanently in Newport, Rhode Island. Again one wonders, in Kidd's mysterious wheelings and dealings, if he purposely first landed at Antigua to make contact with Redwood, alias William Bolton. Or was it, as Kidd indicates, just a fortunate chance meeting at Moona Island, where Kidd persuaded Bolton to rent the **SAINT ANTHONY** to him, so that he might proceed to New England?

Kidd says that, *"I could not persuade my men to carry the* **QUEDAH MERCHANT** *for New England, but six of them went and carried their chests and things on board two Dutch sloops, bound for Curaso; the rest of the men not being able to bring the* **QUEDAH MERCHANT** *prize to Boston. I secured her in a good safe Harbor in some part of Hispaniola, and left her in the possession of Mr. Henry Boulton of Antega, the Master, three of the old men and 16 of the men that belonged to the* **SAINT ANTHONY** *crew, with a Briganteen belonging to a man named Burt of Curaso."* Burt was also a notorious Caribbean pirate, whose real name was Burke. *"I persuaded them to stay three months,"* said Kidd, *"'til I returned, and in the* **SAINT ANTHONY**, *made the best way to New York, where I heard the Earl of Bellomont was in Boston, and came thither. . .".*

There were many important events concerning Kidd and the **SAINT ANTHONY** coming up the East Coast to Boston, which Kidd purposely avoided in his testimony, that were brought out by crewmen and so-called friends during his pre-trial at Boston. There is no doubt that Kidd had transferred much of the treasure from the **QUEDAH MERCHANT** to the **SAINT ANTHONY** before he made his voyage up the coast, but how much, is anybody's guess. Kidd, however, insisted that the bulk of the treasure remained in the **QUEDAH MERCHANT**, hidden in a river at Santo Domingo and protected by some twenty men, *"who await my return."* The first known stop of the **SAINT ANTHONY** on her way to Boston was Lewes, Delaware, where **ADVENTURE GALLEY** crewman James Gillman was put ashore *"with a big wooden chest,"* so another crewman testified. Next, Kidd anchored in Oyster Bay, New York, where he sent a messanger to admiralty attorney James Emmott, who, *"late at night,"* came aboard the **SAINT ANTHONY**. On May 26, 1699, Emmott was in Boston and was received at Peter Sergeant's house, where Richard Coote, the Earl of Bellomont, was staying. Emmott, who Bellomont called, *"a cunning Jacobite,"* told the Governor that *"Kidd is off New England,"* but he wouldn't say exactly where. Emmott handed Bellomont *"sixty pounds of gold and 100 pounds of silver"* from Kidd, and relayed the message that, *"If the Governor would pardon Kidd, he would bring his sloop and treasure to Boston, then go to Hispaniola for the great ship."*

Bellomont's reaction to this information is revealed in a letter he later sent to the members of England's Board of Trade: *"I was puzzled how to manage a treaty of that kind with Emmott,"* he tells them. *"When he proposed my pardoning Kidd, I told him that it was true the King had allowed me a power to pardon pirates, but that I was so tender of using it, because I would bring no stain on my reputation, that I had set myself a rule never to pardon piracy without the King's express leave and command. . . I writ a letter to Captain Kidd inviting him to come in, and that I would procure a pardon for him, provided he were as innocent as Mr. Emmott said he was. I sent my letter to him by one Mr. Campbell of this Town, and a Scotch as well as Kidd, and his acquaintance. . ."*

Duncan Campbell, the Boston Postmaster, who also owned a bookstore in town, was an old friend of Kidd's. At Bellomont's request, he rode out of Boston with Emmott and *"arrived at Rhode Island on Saturday, 17 June, in the morning, and went in a sloop with Emmott towards Block Island. At about three-leagues from that island,"* Campbell reports, *"I met a Sloop commanded by Captain Kidd, and having on board about sixteen men."* Campbell handed Kidd the written pardon from the Governor, which read: *"I have advised with His Majesty's Council* (The Governor's Council) *and showed them this letter, and they are of the opinion that if your case be so clear as you have said, that you may safely come hither, and be equipped and fitted out to obtain the King's pardon for you, and for those few men you have left. I assure you on my word and Honor, I will perform nicely what I have promised, through this I declare beforehand that whatever goods and treasure you may bring hither, I will not meddle with the least bit of them,"* signed, the Earl of Bellomont, Governor of New York, Massachusetts and New Hampshire.

Here is an influencial man, who had paid for most of the expenses of Kidd's expedition, including the vessel that was sunk in St. Maries Harbor and who rightfully owned 75% of Kidd's treasure, telling Kidd that he would *"not meddle the least bit"* with the treasure. Did Kidd know Bellomont well enough to realize that the man was lying through his teeth? Kidd did need the pardon desperately, and Bellomont was his senior partner, but Kidd's next move seems to indicate that he either distrusted Bellomont or decided to hide his treasure to use it as a bargaining chip to gain a pardon from the greedy Governor. Kidd, who promised Campbell, *"you shall have five-hundred pounds for your troubles, when we have our liberty, "* sent his fellow Scotsman back to Boston, telling the Governor that he would soon bring his vessel into that port and file a report condemning the crewmen who had deserted him to take up piracy. Kidd, however, did not sail the **SAINT ANTHONY** to Boston, but went to Gardner's Island. Bellomont tells us that, when Campbell returned to Boston, *"he brought my wife three or four small jewells, which I was to know nothing of, but she came to me and asked whither she should keep them, which I advised her to do, for the present."*

Kidd anchored off Gardner's Island for almost a full week. James Emmott left the sloop and returned to New York City, where he directed Mrs. Kidd and her two daughters to join the Captain aboard the **SAINT ANTHONY.** With them came a pilotboat skipper named Ben Bevins, and four small sloops. John Gardner, owner of the island, also joined Captain Kidd offshore, and treasure chests were taken from Kidd's vessel to these smaller sloops. *"Several chests and packs were put out of Kidd's sloop at Gardner Island,"* crewman Ed Davis reported to the Governor on July 8th at Kidd's pre-trial. *"We believed Kidd's goods were taken off by Carsten Luersten and Hendrick Vanderhead, near Gardner's Island,"* members of the New York Governor's Council informed Bellomont. *"A Major Selleck of Stamford, Connecticut, who has a warehouse close to the Sound,"* Bellomont was informed, *"received at least 10,000 pounds worth of treasure, brought by one Captain Thomas Clark from Kidd's sloop and lodged with Selleck."* The Governor was also told that *"old seaman, Captain Knot of Boston, delivered treasure to Kidd's old mate, Captain Thomas Pain, now living on Canonicot Island at Rhode Island,"* and we know this bit of intelligence was true, for that treasure was discovered under his house by Seth Vose's workmen in 1891. *"Thomas Way of Boston, in his sloop, met Kidd on Nantucket Shoals, on June 30th, after leaving Gardner's Island,"* Ed Davis told the Governor, *"and Kidd gave him bars of gold."* Davis also testified on July 8th, that *"two guns and other East India goods were left at Block Island."*

Kidd, with his wife and daughters and a few crewmen, sailed into Boston Harbor in the **SAINT ANTHONY,** on July 1, 1699, and anchored off shore. He and his family came ashore and stayed at Duncan Campbell's house. The Governor didn't come to see Kidd that day, for *"he was in bed with the gout."* On Monday, July 3rd, Kidd met with the Governor and his Council and was questioned for a few hours. They asked him to submit to them a written report of his three year, supposedly unfortunate, cruise. *"I thought Kidd looked very guilty,"* Bellomont told his Council, *"and to make me believe so, he and Campbell, began to juggle together and embezzle some of the cargo aboard the **SAINT ANTHONY.** Besides, Kidd did strangely trifle with me . . .*

When Kidd landed, I would not so much as speak with him, but before witnesses." When Kidd was not meeting with the Governor and his Council, he delivered to the Governor's wife, the *"Countess of Bellomont,"* a jeweled necklace worth 10,000 pounds sterling. The next day Kidd and his crewmen were questioned again, and the Council insisted on a written report, which Kidd promised for the next day. The report not forthcoming, Kidd was called before the Council again, two days later, and he promised to deliver the report that evening. In the meantime, reports Bellomont, *"Mr. Livingstone came to me in a peremptory manner and demanded his Bond, and the articles which he sealed to me upon Kidd's Expedition, and he told me that Kidd swore an oath that unless I did immediately indemnify Mr. Livingstone by giving up his securities, he, Kidd, would never bring in that great ship and cargo, but would take care to satisfy Mr. Livingstone and himself out of that cargo. I thought this was such an impertinence that it was time for me to secure Captain Kidd. I had noticed that he designed my wife a thousand pounds in gold dust and ingots last Thursday, but I spoiled his complement by ordering him to be arrested and committed that day."* Bellomont said nothing about the jewels and necklace given his wife by Kidd.

Kidd was approached by the Boston Constables outside Peter Sergeant's house, while on his way to see Bellomont, who was living there. Kidd avoided the police by running into the house, but, of course, Bellomont would not protect him, and Kidd was arrested under the Governor's nose. He was placed under house-arrest for a day, then moved to solitary confinement in the Boston Gaol. His hands and feet were cuffed, and the Governor warned that no one was to talk to him. Bellomont didn't trust anyone in Kidd's company, for fear he would bribe them. The Jail Keep and the guards he distrusted most, for they had already allowed notorious pirates to escape Boston Gaol.

Bellomont then had Kidd's vessel searched, but no treasure, only cloth and other merchandise, was found. At Duncan Campbell's house, where Mrs. Kidd and the children were staying, Bellomont's men uncovered six quart bags of gold and one containing silver, plus other *"loose money,"* and in *"Captain Kidd's Box,"* they found *"one quart bag of gold dust and ingots, 53 silver-bars and a quart bag filled with 442 ounces of silver pieces, four diamonds set in gold, one diamond loose, one large diamond set in a gold ring, one emerald and silver box-gilt, and 67 rubies."* Bellomont then sent his men with picks and shovels down to Gardner's Island, where they uncovered eleven bags of gold dust, gold coins, gold ingots, silver bars, coins, buttons, and silver pieces, plus seventeen ounces of diamonds, rubies, and emeralds, valued in those days at about $100,000. Bellomont also, *"posted away a message to Rhode Island Governor Cranston and Colonel Stanford to make a strict search of old pirate Captain Thomas Pain's house at Canonicot Island, before he could have notice."* Bellomont later reported that, *"It seems nothing was found at Pain's house, but Pain has since produced eighteen ounces of gold, as appears by Governor Cranston's letter, and he pretends it was bestowed on him by Kidd... I am of opinion he has a great deal more of Kidd's goods still in his hands."* How right Bellomont was, for the treasure sat deep in the dirt under Pain's house for 192 years— apparently Pain just couldn't spend it all in his lifetime.

Bellomont also sent a message to the authorities in Connecticut to *"Seize and send Thomas Clark a prisoner to New York,"* accused of *"transporting Kidd's crew and treasure into Connecticut Colony."* Bellomont also had Major Selleck's warehouse at Stamford searched, but none of Kidd's treasure was found there. Thomas *"Whisking"* Clark was soon released from the New York Jail, and no one has seen or heard from him since.

Kidd's explanation for all this treasure found, or unfound, by Bellomont's men, was summed up in a letter to the Governor: *"The gold that was seized at Mr. Campbell's, I traded for at Madagascar, with what came out of the ADVENTURE GALLEY. Some of my sloop's company put two bales of goods on shore at Gardner's Island, being their own property. I delivered chests of goods, muslins, latches, silk, and romols* (handkerchiefs) *into Mr. Gardiner, to be kept there for me, but put no goods on shore anywhere else."* It's obvious, from the treasure found under the Pain-Vose house in 1891, that Kidd is lying. However, Kidd goes on to say that, *"several of my Company landed their chests and other goods at several places. I delivered a small bayle of calicoes unto a sloop of Rhode Island that I had employed there. The gold seized at Mr. Campbell's I intended for presents to some that I expected to do me kindness. Some of my Company put their chests and bayles on board a New York sloop lying at Gardner's Island."* — Who are we to believe?

After Bellomont's informal pre-trial of Captain Kidd, where conflicting evidence confused the issue even further, and stimulated rumor by New Englanders that their Governor was as guilty of piracy as Kidd, he decided to transfer Kidd's trial to England. A Massachusetts law, passed in 1693, after the Witchtrial Hysteria, made it illegal to punish witches, vagabonds, or pirates with death. So, to get rid of the responsibility of Kidd and to enhance the possibilities that he might hang as a pirate, Bellomont shipped him across the ocean in chains to Newgate Gaol. He languished in jail for almost two years and then was tried at the Old Baily on May 9, 1701. Kidd pleaded that, *"I took no other ships but enemy ships that had French Passes, which I brought with me to New England."* But in Boston, Lord Bellomont had taken these passes from him, and failed to send them on to England for the trial. If the passes were produced, Kidd realized, it would be difficult to convict him of piracy. *"Lord Bellomont has kept these passes wholly from me,"* he told the magistrates, *"and has stript me of all defence,"* but the English Judges didn't care, and they decided not to convict Kidd of piracy anyway — they got him for the murder of William Moore. Prior to Kidd's conviction, his old royal partners in the Expedition, the Earl of Orford, First Lord of the Admiralty, and Sir John Somers, Chancellor and Lord Keeper of the Great Seal, were also tried for gaining unlawfully from their positions and for being in partnership with Kidd. They were found guilty and impeached. Lord Bellomont feared that he would be next.

Bellomont however, kept British authorities informed about his on-going quest to find the bulk of Kidd's treasure. *"I am running out a ship to go for the QUEDAH MERCHANT,"* he wrote to the Board of Trade in August of 1699. *"By some papers which we seized with Kidd, and by his own confession, we have found out where the ship lyes, and according to his account of the cargo, we compute her to be worth seventy thousand pounds."* Abraham Redwood, alias William Bolton, wrote to Bellomont, under a new pseudonym, Henry Bolton, saying he wanted his sloop **SAINT ANTONIO** back and that Kidd had only rented it. Kidd called the sloop **SAINT ANTHONY**. Bolton revealed to the Governor that, *"after the departure of Captain Kidd from the West Indies, the seamen shipped by him in the QUEDAH MER-CHANT, did plunder her, and convert to their own uses the best and most choicest of the goods and cargo, which did not come to my knowledge for five weeks, and it was out of my power to prevent them. They were eighteen in number, and they left the ship for Curacao."*

The most prominent person that Kidd left at Hispaniola with the **QUEDAH MERCHANT**, was *"a man named Burt of Curaso."* Burt was an Irish pirate, noted for his piratical activities in the Caribbean, whose real name was Burke. It's interesting to note that Bellomont, in November 1699, after the **QUEDAH MERCHANT** was supposedly robbed of her treasure by the men left in charge of her, writes that, *"Burke, an Irishman and pirate that committed several robberies on the coast of Newfoundland, is drowned with all of his ship's Company, except seven or eight persons, somewhere to the Southward. It is* said he perished in a hurricane that was in these Seas about the beginning of August last. It is good news, for he was very strong, if we can believe the report, and is said to have had a good ship with a 140 man crew and twenty-four guns." Did Burke take the treasure from Kidd's ship? Did he really drown in a storm? It seems that the more we learn about Kidd, and his friends and enemies, the more the true story is clouded in mystery.

Rear-Admiral Benbow, still cruising the West Indies in October, 1699, writes to the British Board of Trade that, "At Saint Thomas Island, a great part of Kidd's cargo was protected by the Governor. He says he will trade with any, and be accountable to none but his master. The Governor has now several things in his possession which came out of Kidd, and also a great quantity of money." Did Kidd make a deal with the Governor of Saint Thomas too? Kidd said that the Governor there treated him poorly, and so, unless one of the **QUEDAH MERCHANT** crew who Kidd left behind made a deal with the Saint Thomas Governor, we must assume that Kidd was lying again. Shortly after Admiral Benbow's revelation, Captain Nicholas Evertse of New York, while sailing out of St. Katherina, Hispaniola, reported seeing "the QUEDAH MERCHANT on fire and burnt to the waterline" on a lagoon at Saona Island, off the southern end of Santo Domingo. Evertse said that he saw the great treasure ship sink on June 29, less than three months after Kidd left the Caribbean in the **SAINT ANTHONY**.

As late as March 6, 1700, Bellomont is writing to the Board of Trade stating that, "I am continuing my search for the treasure which Kidd brought upon the coast, but without much success." Lord Bellomont died shortly thereafter, either of frustration at not finding Kidd's treasure, or from fear that he would himself go before the British Magistrates and "bring a stain on my reputation."

Kidd never revealed to Bellomont and the English authorities, nor apparently to his partner Livingstone either, that he buried the most precious jewels and gold items from his two "Moorish prizes," somewhere on an island in New England, sometime between May 20th and July 1st, 1699. "It is made up in a bag," said Darby Mullins, before he was hanged with Kidd, "put into a little box, locked and nailed, corded about and sealed," but Darby wouldn't say where Kidd's personal treasure in the "little box" was buried. On May 23, 1701, neither Kidd nor Mullins were thinking about treaure. On that day they were marched out of Newgate Gaol and for three hours, were pushed and shoved by a drunken mob, who shouted at them to reveal where the treasure was hidden, until they arrived under guard at Execution Dock on the muddy flats of the Thames River at Wapping. By the time they got to the gallows, at 3 p.m., both Kidd and Mullins were roaring drunk, having been fed spirits along the route by the celebrating crowd— it was a workman's holiday at Wapping, aptly called, *"The Hangman's Fair."* Staggering, with the rope around his neck, Kidd blurted, *"My Lord, this is a very hard sentence. For my part, I am innocent, and I have been sworn against by perjured persons."* The trap-door of the staging was released and Kidd fell through, but the rope broke and Kidd landed knee-deep in the mudflats. The crowd went wild, cheering and laughing, and they extracted him from the mud, still alive and still drunk. The crowd protested when the constables escorted him back to the gallows for a second try — the broken rope indicated God's judgement that Kidd was innocent, so most in the crowd believed, but he was nevertheless hanged again successfully this second time, and Mullins soon followed him into eternity.

And so, the songs, poems and legends began, and the man who swore to his dying day that he wasn't a pirate, became the most famous pirate in the world. After death, his body was painted with tar and gibbetted in chains on the river bank at Tilbury Fort, for all mariners to see and reflect on as they came and went on the sea. Even without his supposedly ill-gotten goods, Captain Kidd died a wealthy man, and his family was well cared for financially. One strange quirk of fate that made him even richer, was that his best friend and brother-in-law, Samuel Bradley, who sailed with him in the **ADVENTURE GALLEY** and **QUEDAH MERCHANT**, died before Kidd was hanged. He had been put ashore by Kidd at Anguilla because he was sick and feverish, and there he soon died. In his will, he left his *"beloved friend William Kidd,"* all his property on New York City's Wall Street. If Kidd had lived, he would have owned more than half of America's famed financial district.

Still in private circulation throughout the world, but especially in New England and Nova Scotia, are what is known as, *"The Kidd-Palmer Charts."* They are treasure maps, secreted in various places, supposedly by Captain Kidd before he was executed. Hubert and Guy Palmer, brothers and noted attornies in Sussex, England during the early part of this century, also were avid collectors of authentic pirate paraphenalia. In 1931, they discovered one of these controversial *"charts"* in a secret drawer of a 17th century oak bureau that they had purchased at auction. *"Wrapped in a brass tube, hidden in this secret compartment,"* Hubert reveals, *"was a nautical chart of the China Seas,"* which denoted an island there, where Kidd hid his treasure, apparently some time shortly after the mutiny of his men at Madagascar. This chart was the incentive for Richard Knight and Fred Graham to go searching for Kidd's treasure at Phu Quoc, Vietnam in 1983. Others had attempted and failed before them. In 1933, the Palmer brothers bought an old sea-chest from a Pamela Hardy of Jersey, whose ancestor, Captain Thomas Hardy of the **H.M.S. VICTORY**, had taken from pirate Ned Ward, Kidd's boatswain mate aboard the **ADVENTURE GALLEY**. The Palmers discovered a false bottom in this chest, which contained a piece of parchment with the sketch of an island on it. Marked in red ink in the middle of the island-sketch, was an "x" and written, *"Kidd's Treasure,"* but there is no indication where this island is located.

Another sea-chest that the Palmers acquired that same year had the inscription *"William & Sarah Kidd — Their Box,"* carved into it. This chest also contained a secret compartment and the drawing of an island-map on old parchment. Although it was a different island, it showed the locations of eight catches of buried treasure belonging to Kidd. Again, there are no longitude and latitude markings on this map, so there is no way of knowing where this island is. The Palmer brothers are now dead, but two cartographers have deemed *"The Kidd-Palmer Charts"* as genuine. Many treasure hunters today use these charts in an attempt to find those special treasure islands, searching everywhere from Canada, New England and New York to the West Indies. No one yet, to my knowledge, has found the islands that fit the shapes and topography of Kidd's sketches. The maps may, however, be fakes, but if so, treasure hunters should not be too upset. After all, the old game of pirating was one in which lies and deception were the rule, and no one knew that better, or played the game harder, than a wealthy merchant adventurer named William Kidd.

V
SECRETS OF THE SHOALS

A little cluster of seven rocky islands and adjoining reefs, called The Isles of Shoals is New Hampshire's only claim to salt water islands. Even that claim is somewhat spoiled, for the state of Maine, which boasts 2,000 offshore islands, cuts right through them. Squatting out there, ten miles off the coast of Portsmouth, they can be seen from the mainland of three states on a clear day. Since fishermen settled there in pre-Pilgrim days, Maine, Massachusetts, and New Hampshire have argued over their ownership. *"The islanders,"* writes New Hampshire historian Lyman Rutledge, *"many times refused to pay taxes to anyone.... Shoalers were always against Massachusetts government,"* he says, *"and in 1652, were considered separate from Mass Bay."* Still divided, north and south, between Maine and New Hampshire, three of the islands are now connected by breakwaters. In the 17th and early 18th centuries, *"the Anglicans were on the north island and the Puritans in the south village."* Even with this strong religious division, however, writes Rutledge, *"some kept switching islands to get from one jurisdiction to another."*

Best known of the Isles' historians is Celia Thaxter, who was brought up there in the mid 1800's. *"At the time of the first settlement,"* she writes, *"the islands were infested by pirates."* John Scribner Jenness, historian of the previous century writes, *"there is strong ground for suspicion, indeed, that the Islanders were generally indulgent and sometimes friendly and serviceable in their intercourse with the numerous pirate ships which visited their harbor."* One islander who befriended pirates, and probably was a pirate himself, was Philip Babb. Legend has it that he was one of Captain Kidd's mates, but he couldn't have been, for he died at the Isles in 1671. *"He is supposed to have been so desperately wicked when alive,"* writes Celia Thaxter, *"that there is no rest for him in his grave. His dress is coarse,"* she says of his spirit, *"a striped butcher's frock, with a leather belt, to which is attached a sheath containing a ghostly knife, sharp and glittering, which is his delight to brandish in the face of terrified humanity."* Babb lived on Appledore, the largest of the Isles, half a mile long and almost as wide. His house was on a hill on the south side of the island, near the cove. Here, he dug a large pit with his friend Ambrose Gibbon in which he supposedly found a large treasure chest. It was too heavy to lift out of the pit, and *"smoke came from its lid when they tried to break the lock,"* writes Oscar Leighton, another Isles historian. There was also the smell of sulphur, which forced them to leave the chest. Obviously, much of Babb's shady life is cloaked in legend, but all historians agree that Babb did dig a great hole near the cove at Appledore Island. *"It was filled in during the great storm of 1851,"* writes Leighton, and *"a Coast Guard boathouse was later built over the treasure pit."* Babb's ghost, of course, guards the buried treasure chest, so it seems wiser that modern day treasure hunters concentrate on pirate catches that are known to be buried at the Isles, and are not haunted by a demented butcher.

Pirate Captain Jack Quelch was a butcher of another sort, for his creed was to kill everyone aboard any vessel he captured and looted. Members of his blood-thirsty crew were actually caught in the act of burying gold at the Isles. His piratical career lasted only a year, having begun when he was first officer aboard the privateer **CHARLES** out of Boston. The 88-ton brigantine **CHARLES** was commissioned by Governor Joseph Dudley, on July 13, 1703, with the intent to, *"war, fight, kill, suppress, and destroy any Pyrates, Privateers, or other Subjects and Vassals of Spain or France, and declared enemies of England..."* She sailed on her maiden voyage, twelve short miles from Boston to Marblehead, for her commander, Daniel Plowman, found it impossible to recruit enough crewmen at Boston. After Captain Kidd's experience, few seamen wanted to join pirate hunting expeditions. Even Captain Plowman seemed a bit reluctant. From his anchorage off Marblehead, he wrote to the ship owners in Boston to *"give up the enterprise,"* for the few seamen he was able to hire at Marblehead did not seem to be *"honest sailors."* One of the owners came to Marblehead to talk to Plowman, but at the Town Landing, he was greeted by **CHARLES** crewman Anthony Holding, who told him that the *"Captain is in his cabin, too sick for visitors."* Frustrated, the owner returned to Boston, where he received a second letter from Plowman, admitting that he was *"in poor health,"* and that *"a new Captain should take Command,"* but to *"do so quickly... and take speedy care in saving what we can... in order to prevent embezzlement."* The owner rushed back to Marblehead, but was two hours too late — the **CHARLES** had sailed.

Off Halfway Rock, the last island passed on the way to sea from Marblehead, Captain Plowman was dragged out of his cabin and thrown overboard. Some of the **CHARLES** crew later testified that Plowman had died from sickness before he was dropped overboard, but others claimed that he was still alive. Leader of the mutinous crew was Anthony Holding. The crew soon decided that Quelch should be their leader. He accepted the responsibility, ordering the helmsman to steer for the East coast of South America. They took their first prize, a large Portuguese brig, off Brazil. Though she carried twelve cannons, they captured her with little resistance. Cruising the coast, the **CHARLES** pirates took four more Portuguese brigantines in quick succession, then a shallop, a ship, and two sloops. By March of 1704, they had pirated 17 vessels, and had collected some 200 pounds weight of gold dust, over 200 silver bars, and a quantity of fine gems. Although none of the vessels they pirated were Spanish, Quelch reported that, on the way back to New England, they encountered a Spanish galleon foundering on a West Indian reef, *"and salvaged much of her cargo of silver and gold."* On May 20, 1704, Quelch and his crew boldly sailed the **CHARLES** back into Marblehead Harbor and anchored. In the dead of night, all of them, carrying heavy canvas bags and wooden chests, abandoned ship and dispersed.

There is speculation, even to this day, that the **CHARLES** anchored at Gosport Harbor at the Isles of Shoals, prior to coming into Marblehead, and that the heavy 200 or more silver bars were buried on the west side of Appledore Island. While building a seawall at Smuttynose Island, Isles of Shoals, in 1816, Sam Haley Jr. uncovered four silver bars in the sand of South Beach, which were thought at the time to be part of Quelch's buried treasure. Many Marbleheaders believe that much of the treasure was buried only a few hundred feet from their Town Landing. In fact, *"Treasure Hunters Day"* was celebrated in May of each year in Marblehead, well into the 20th century.

No information on pirate treasure from the **CHARLES** would have been forthcoming, had not some members of the crew, the day after their arrival, frequented Marblehead taverns, spending gold doubloons and nuggets of gold dust for drinks, *"and whilst in their cups,"* divulged to tavern wenches, *"the great riches of Portuguese cargoes they had taken off Brazil."* Word quickly reached Boston and the ear of Governor Dudley. Constables were sent out to scour the inns and taverns, favorite ports-of-call for thirsty pirates, and Captain Jack Quelch was arrested, without resistance, at the Anchor Tavern in Lynn, Massachusetts. Quelch insisted that he was on the way to Boston to inform the owners of the **CHARLES** that he had arrived home with Spanish treasure. He avoided mentioning the Portuguese vessels he had robbed, for in the tavern he had heard that England had, in his absence, signed a peace treaty with Portugal. He was brought before Paul Dudley, the Governor's son, who also happened to be the Attorney General of the Colony. When Dudley accused him of piracy, Quelch insisted that Captain Plowman had ordered him to take command before he died and, by direction of Plowman, he had sailed for Brazil. Quelch almost managed to convince the Attorney General and the owners of the **CHARLES** that he wasn't a pirate, but when other members of the crew were rounded up they contradicted the Captain. Quelch was tossed into Boston Gaol. Of the 42 pirate crewmen aboard the **CHARLES**, Dudley's constables captured seven within two days — *"carrying on their persons, 45 ounces of gold and gold coins."* John Clifford, one of the pirates, agreed to tell the Attorney General everything about their voyage, if he was pardoned. He confessed that after arriving at Marblehead, *"a considerable quantity of gold dust and gems was put out from Salem to Cape Anne, with Captain Thomas Larimore in the LARIMORE GALLEY, with eleven or more of Captain Quelch's Company."* The Governor called out the militia, and a regiment under Colonel Legg of Marblehead, saddled up and headed for Gloucester, while Major Stephen Sewall and twenty militiamen sailed to Cape Ann from Marblehead. Scuttlebut at Gloucester was that the **LARIMORE GALLEY** was anchored off shore at Snake Island. At Snake Island, a fisherman informed Major Sewall that the pirates had sailed for the Isles of Shoals, only an hour or two before he had arrived off Gloucester.

Sailing the twenty miles to the Isles, and spying the **LARIMORE GALLEY** anchored off Star Island, Sewall had his men hide in the cabin of his shallop. He pulled along side the **LARIMORE**, pretending he was a fisherman. Then, on his signal, his militiamen boarded her, expecting a battle. To their surprise, there were only Tom Larimore and a 14 year old boy aboard the **LARIMORE GALLEY**. The others were ashore at the Isles, burying their individual shares of treasure. The militiamen rowed ashore and, one by one, subdued seven pirates, some still carrying bags of gold dust. They transported them and their gold, with Captain Larimore, back to Boston Jail. Pirate Matt Primer informed Major Sewall where six more of the **CHARLES** crew were hiding out, in exchange for a pardon, and these pirates were also rounded up by constables at various seaside villages and towns. In all, twenty five of the **CHARLES** crew, including Quelch, were captured and jailed, but eighteen, including ringleader Anthony Holding, were never caught.

Governor Dudley was the presiding magistrate at the pirates' trial, which lasted from June 13th to June 21st. Three who *"turned evidence,"* were pardoned, 15 who pleaded guilty but were repentent, were shipped off to England for life sentences as soldiers in the British Army, and seven, including Jack Quelch, were *"condemned to hang for murder and piracy."* On June 30, 1704, they were marched under guard of forty men from the jail to Boston's Scarlett Wharf where, *"in the Charles River, between high and low water, a gallows had been erected."* Judge Samuel Sewall, who was at the execution, writes in his diary that, *"the river was covered with people in a hundred boats and canoes. When the scaffold was hoisted to a due height, the seven Malafactors went up. Ropes were fastened to the gallows, save for Francis King, who was reprieved."* Reverend Cotton Mather, when executing pirates, always liked to save one life at the last minute— Mather then, in a long speech, begged the condemned pirates to repent. Quelch spoke up, *"I am not afraid of death, but I am afraid of what follows. I am condemned only upon circumstances, but all should take care how they bring money into New England, to be hanged for it."* The crowd cheered and Quelch bowed to them, as if he were on stage. When the *"scaffold was let to sink,"* Sewall writes, *"there was such a screech from the women present, that my wife heard it sitting in our orchard, and was much surprised, for our house is a full mile from the hanging place."*

Quelch and two of the others were cut down next day, their bodies chained and limbs cuffed. They were gibbeted at Nix's Mate, a small island in Boston Harbor off Winthrop, on display for years as a warning to other seamen who might be tempted into piracy. The others were turned over to the students of Harvard for biological study and dissection. There was, of course, still the question of the treasure. Governor Dudley and his son had reclaimed 65 pounds of gold dust from captured pirates, most of it from the seven who were caught as they were burying it at the Isles of Shoals. While in jail, Quelch had told Cotton Mather that the Governor was going to hang him because *"I wouldn't share my gold dust with him,"* the Governor being well aware that the 65 pounds of gold dust captured was only a fraction of what the pirates had brought back from Brazil. Mather called Governor Dudley, *"a trecherous man who deals with pirates,"* and insinuated that some of the confiscated gold dust had *"stuck to his fingers."* The *"silver bars, coins and gems,"* and the rest of the gold dust, was never uncovered. It is thought to still be buried either at Snake Island off Cape Ann, somewhere near Marblehead Landing, or, (since Sewall caught some of them burying it there) at Star Island, on the Isles of Shoals.

One who didn't heed the message of Quelch's rotting body, gibbeted in Boston Harbor, was Sandy Gordon, a crewman aboard Captain John Herring's British ship **PORPOISE**. Captain Herring had his teenaged daughter aboard the **PORPOISE**. In the summer of 1714, during a long Atlantic cruise, Sandy Gordon was discovered by the Captain in an uncompromising position with young Martha, in her cabin. Sandy's punishment was 72 lashes of the whip, which almost killed him. When his wounds had healed a few weeks later, Sandy sought revenge, and persuaded part of the **PORPOISE** crew to mutiny. Seizing the ship, Sandy and ten men killed all crewmen who remained loyal to the Captain, then he strapped Martha's father to the mast and gave him 72 lashes of the whip, which did kill the Captain. After taking three English merchant vessels off the coast of Scotland, Captain Sandy Gordon refused to share the little treasure they confiscated from these vessels with his mutinous crew, so they mutinied again, and this time Sandy was the victim. They didn't kill their short-lived commander, but put him ashore on an island off Scotland with Martha Herring. The crew then sailed away in the **PORPOISE**.

Living in a fisherman's shanty for many months, Sandy and Martha one day spotted a fleet of four ships offshore. They were pirate vessels. When the pirates came ashore to the island for water, Sandy talked to them, and was invited aboard their flagship to talk to the Commadore of the fleet. Here he met and joined forces with a man already infamous as *"The Terror of the Sea,"* a six foot six inch giant, sporting a two foot beard, with pistols and a cutlass tucked into his wide waist-belt. It was Ed Teach, alias Blackbeard. Blackbeard apparently got a kick out of Sandy's plight of being marooned by the **PORPOISE** crew, so he allowed Sandy to join him. Sailing the Atlantic, the pirate fleet captured a French brig and a Spanish galleon containing over $1,000,000 in gold and silver, on its way to the King of Spain. The French brig was renamed the **FLYING SCOT** by Blackbeard, and given to Sandy Gordon to command, as a reward for his bravado in the fight with the French and Spaniards. The pirate vessels were now so filled with treasure that Blackbeard decided to head for the nearest landfall to rid themselves of some of it — the nearest landfall, a port where pirates were welcomed, was New Hampshire's Isles of Shoals.

Again, as with Philip Babb, the story of Blackbeard and Sandy Gordon at the Isles, has been mixed with legend over the last 270 years. It is said that there was a great ceremony and celebration at Star Island when Sandy Gordon married Martha Herring, and that same day, Blackbeard married a girl he had aboard his 40-gun ship **QUEEN ANNE'S REVENGE**. Blackbeard never took marriage seriously however, for during his lifetime he had 14 wives, and never went to sea without a bevy of concubines. When he was killed in 1718, 40 children claimed him as their father. Sandy and Martha did take their marriage vows seriously and settled at White Island, one of the Isles, but their honeymoon was brief. The English Navy had been searching the

Atlantic for the **PORPOISE** mutineers for over a year. A man-of-war came to the Isles shortly after Sandy and Martha set up housekeeping on White Island. Blackbeard, after staying at Star Island for over a month, wisely set sail and left the Isles, but Gordon in the **FLYING SCOT**, went out to battle the naval warship. Two well directed broadsides and the **FLYING SCOT** sank like a rock, with Sandy Gordon, in his favorite bright red uniform, going down with her. Supposedly, only two of the pirate crew survived the sinking, and they were picked up by the man-of-war crew and hanged at the yardarm that very day. The only member of the pirate-band left at the Isles was Martha Herring Gordon, who died there in 1735. Celia Thaxter writes, *"Teach's comrade, Captain Scott(Gordon), brought this lovely lady hither. They buried immense treasure on the islands; that of Scott(Gordon) was buried on an island apart from the rest... The maiden was carried to the island where her pirate lover's treasure was hidden, and made to swear with horrible rites, that until his return, if it were not till the day of judgement, she would guard it from search of all mortals. So, there she paces still... She laments like a Banshee before the tempest, wailing through the gorges at Appledore."*

Blackbeard and his men, forced to quickly depart the Isles and never return, *"buried their treasure on Smuttynose and Londoner Islands,"* wrote one Isles historian. Londoner Island is now called Lunging Island. *"Blackbeard's treasure is buried at the landing side of the beach facing the Star Island Hotel, halfway across the half moon stretch of beach,"* writes another historian, and a third says Blackbeard's treasure is hidden, *"just below the waterline on the beach east of the breakwater at Smuttynose."* Blackbeard himself, however, was quoted as saying, *"Nobody but the devil and myself knows where my treasure is."*

Blackbeard sailed to Rhode Island and Connecticut, stopping at Providence and New London. At the latter port, it is said that he and his men took a long trek, with some of their treasure, up the Nipmuck Trail and entered Providence, supposedly burying their treasure along the way, near the border of the two Colonies, possibly at Hampton or Brooklyn, Connecticut. A man named Cady of Hampton reported in 1938, that one of Ed Teach's descendants, a Barny Reynolds, came to Hampton and uncovered part of the treasure. According to Mr. Cady, Reynolds had a map, *"which he inherited from Blackbeard."*

From New England, Blackbeard returned to his base of operations at Bath, North Carolina. After taking some forty vessels off America's East Coast, Governor Spotswood of Virginia offered 100 pounds for the *"apprehending and killing of Edward Teach, commonly called*

Blackbeard. " In November of 1718, two British naval sloops under the command of Lieutenant Maynard, and with the help of former pirate Basil Hand, cornered Blackbeard and his crew off the Carolina coast. Blackbeard and 22 men fought furiously, boarding the British sloops and fighting the sailors in hand-to-hand combat. Most of the pirates, including the wild and wooly pirate commander, were killed— Blackbeard received five musketballs in the head and some twenty stab wounds. Finally, Maynard sliced his throat. Blackbeard's head was delivered to the Governor on a pole.

Early in his career, Blackbeard served under Captain Benjamin Hornigold, a noted Caribbean pirate, as did one Sam *"Black"* Bellamy. Blackbeard and Black Bellamy left Hornigold, for the latter refused to attack or loot English vessels. Bellamy, commanding a fleet of three pirate vessels, including his flagship, the English galley **WHYDAH**, were off the New England coast in April of 1717, when a wild storm drove the **WHYDAH** ashore on Cape Cod. Bellamy along with some 100 pirates went down with their ship— only two crewmen climbed the sand cliffs to safety. The **MARY ANN**, a prize of the **WHYDAH**, grounded off Chatham, Massachusetts in the storm, and seven of Bellamy's pirates tried to escape capture by walking to Rhode Island. They were caught by the Cape Cod Sheriff and escorted to Boston Gaol. At the time, Blackbeard threatened to attack Boston with some 500 pirates to free Bellamy's men, but he never put his plan into action. As a result, the pirates were hanged, with only one being reprieved at the last minute by Cotton Mather.

One of Bellamy's pirate ships escaped the storm however, and according to the testimonies of Ralph Merry and Samuel Roberts, on May 16, 1717, these 19 pirates attacked their sloop **FISHER** *"a few leagues off Cape Cod,"* and took them prisoners. They took another sloop off Gloucester, then sailed on to Monhegan Island, Maine. John Newman of Gloucester later reported that the pirates had *"several chests, trunks, and bale goods aboard their sloop."* From Monhegan, they moved on to Matinicus Island, south of Rockland, Maine and pirated three more vessels, *"a Shallop belonging to Stephen Minot of Boston. . . and two Shallops from Marblehead."* The pirates then released their prisoners and headed for the Isles of Shoals, where nothing more was heard of them.

Blackbeard and Black Bellamy weren't as wise as their old commander Ben Hornigold. He got to enjoy his treasure. Hornigold surrendered himself to the Governor of Bermuda, under the King's Proclamation of September 5, 1717, which offered a pardon to all pirates, and unlike his pirate pals, he lived happily ever after. Two other pirate leaders with ties to the Isles of Shoals, who didn't take advantage of the King's Pardon, were Ned Low and William Fly. Although the King and Parliament hoped to rid the seas of buccaneers with the 1717 Proclamation, pirate terrorism off the coast of New England increased dramatically in the following ten years.

Many have searched for Ned Low's treasure at the Isles, supposedly buried at either Duck Island or Smuttynose, and also, said to be buried at Pond Island, one of the Harpswell Isles in Casco Bay, Maine. After attacking the Spanish galleon **DON PEDRO DEL MONTCLOVA**, and confiscating *"kettles of silver bars and a chest of gold and jewels,"* reported one of his crew, Low rowed ashore from his pirate ship and deposited this great treasure in a marshy fresh water pond at Pond Island, Maine. Apparently, while dumping the treasure, the pirates got into an argument and then a sword fight. Two pirates were killed, and Ned Low, often referred to as *"a psycopathic killer,"* left the bodies in the pond with the treasure. According to Orr and Bailey Islanders, *"the water turned bad after Low's visit."* The marshy pond is dried up today, but at the north end of Pond Island Cove, someone might some day dig up Low's gold, silver and jewels.

Low was killed, *"set adrift to die of thirst,"* by his own crew a few weeks after his Pond Island deposit, mainly because his men just couldn't stand him any longer. He started his career at Grand Cayman Island in the West Indies, when he met up with pirate George Lowther. Lowther, an Englishman, had led a mutiny at Gambia and took over the ship **HAPPY DELIVERY**, which he sailed to the West Indies to take up pirating. The first ship that he and his crew attacked was the brigantine **CHARLES** of Boston, bound for Barbadoes. Succeeding, he took six more vessels off Hispaniola, then went to Cayman, a favorite food and water stop for pirates. Low, with 13 men who had recently mutinied, also was at Cayman *"for water and turtles."* Lowther invited Low to join forces and they headed for New England to raise havoc during the Summer of 1722.

Low forced capable seamen into piracy from all the ships he boarded. Those who refused to join him were beaten up— some were killed. Three fishermen whom he captured off the Isles of Shoals, later reported that Low said he would hang them, *"unless ye jump up and down and curse the name of Doctor Cotton Mather."* On June 15th, at Port Roseway, Nova Scotia, Low and his men captured 14 vessels in that one day. Among the seamen captured was 19 year old Philip Ashton of Marblehead. *"Captain Low asked me to be a pirate,"* Ashton later reported, *"but I told him 'No'. He threatened to shoot me, but I refused their drink as well as their proposals, so the pirate captain put me in chains below."* Ashton writes that, *"some of the prisoners were allowed to leave at the Isles of Shoals,"* but he was kept in chains, as Low's little fleet continued to pirate vessels off New England. *"I was beaten and whipped,"* says Ashton, *"and I begged Low on my knees to let me go, but he said 'No'. . . and I was taken to the West Indies."*

Back in their winter retreat, the pirate crew with Ashton aboard, anchored off a jungle island near Honduras, and Ashton was allowed to go ashore for water— he ran and hid in the jungle until the pirate ship left the island five days later. Eating *"figs, coconuts, papayas, turtles, snakes, lizards, crabs, and birds,"* Ashton survived on Roatan Island for 16 months, until the brigantine **DIAMOND** of Salem, Captain Dove commanding, came to the island for water and Ashton was rescued. In the meantime, Captain Lowther in the **HAPPY DELIVERY**, was attacked by the armed sloop **EAGLE** at Blanco Island near Tortuga. Lowther was careening his ship and his cannons weren't set. The **EAGLE** blasted the pirates with broadsides, and they fled into the surrounding jungle. The **EAGLE** crew pursued them, capturing 20 pirates and saving seven forced men. Lowther himself was found in the jungle four days later — he had committed suicide. All but six of the pirates were hanged, and the forced men, like Philip Ashton, were returned to their homes. Ned Low, however, avoided the confrontation with the **EAGLE**. He and his men were happily and successfully pirating ships, including the rich galleon **MONTCOVA**, aboard which Low slaughtered 53 Spaniards. His own crew then decided to get rid of him— that was the end of Ned Low.

Another *"ferocious brute of unequalled cruelty,"* who also had a fondness for the Isles of Shoals, was William Fly. Like Ned Low, he seemed to have a dual personality, kind to a seaman one moment, torturing or slicing his throat the next. His career beginning two years after Low's ended, in 1726, and began and ended much like Low's did. A mutiny aboard the slave ship **ELIZABETH** of England was led by the boatswain, Bill Fly. The captain of the **ELIZABETH**, John Green, while being thrown overboard far at sea, *"grabbed for the lines, but pirate Tom Winthrop cut off his hands."* Then the first mate Jenkins was thrown into the sea and Fly became the **ELIZABETH**'s pirate commander. He changed the ship's name to **FAME'S REVENGE**. Off the Carolina coast, Fly and his crew took four vessels, one being the **RACHEL** from Ireland, with 50 immigrants aboard. Fly robbed them all of their life savings, and from each of his prizes, forced crewmen to join his pirate crew.

The **FAME'S REVENGE** then sailed for Martha's Vineyard and on to Cape Ann, where they captured the ship **JAMES**. The **JAMES** was converted into a pirate vessel, and with most of the pirate crew aboard her, began attacking fishing vessels off the Isles of Shoals. As Cotton Mather reveals in his book, *"The Vial Poured Out Upon The Sea,"* Captain Fly *"wanted all the fishing schooners."* Watching his men in the **JAMES** loot the schooners, as he stood on the deck of **FAME'S REVENGE**, Fly made the mistake of allowing two forced men aboard his ship to watch the piracy through his spyglass. The two men grabbed Fly and held him, while *"Atkinson the navigator, who Fly previously threatened to kill, with two others, got a gun aft on the quarterdeck, and made Fly surrender."* There were twelve forced men, including Atkinson, aboard the **FAME'S REVENGE**, and they took over the ship, sailing straight for Boston. The **JAMES** crew tried to catch them, but couldn't. The **JAMES** then sailed for the Isles of Shoals, and like many previous pirate crews, they disbanded there — these lucky pirates aboard the **JAMES** were never captured.

Fly and three of his men were jailed and stood trial at the old Boston Statehouse on July 4, 1726 — his career had lasted only 35 days. William Fly, who had whipped one Captain Fulker of the sloop **JOHN & HANNAH**, *"until blood filled his shoes,"* carried a newly plucked rose with him to the gallows, laughing and joking with the great crowd that had gathered. According to Cotton Mather, Fly said to the obviously nervous hangman, *"you don't know your own trade, and then he helped the hangman tie the knot."* The Boston News-Letter reported that, *"Fly advised Masters of vessels not to be severe and barbarous to their men, which might be a reason why so many turned pirates. . . ."* Fly and his crewmen Samuel Cole and Henry Greenville were hanged, but pirate George Condick was reprieved the last minute by Mather.

"Their bodies were carried in a boat to a small island called Nick's Mate, about two leagues from the Town," reports the Boston News-Letter, *"where the above said Fly was hung up in irons, as a spectacle for the warning of others, especially seafaring men; the other two were buried there."* Legend has it that this island, once covering some 13 acres in Boston Harbor, suddenly sank to a size of one quarter acre when an accused pirate was hanged there in 1698. His name is lost to history, but he swore he was innocent, and to prove his innocence, the island would sink after his hanging — which it did. He had been the first-mate aboard a Captain Nix's vessel, and thus the name — Nix's Mate Island. It used to be called Bird Island. A 32-foot high concrete pyra-

mid, supported by 16-foot square walls, topped with a beacon, is all that remains of Nix's Mate Island today.

Another pirate gibbeted at Nix's Mate was William Phillips, who was also captured off the Isles of Shoals, two years before William Fly. He was a typical pirate type, one-legged and full of curses. William Phillips was a crewman aboard Commander John Philip's pirate ship, which captured 34 New England fishing sloops and schooners in 1723. The following May, however, Phillips and Philip, made the mistake of pirating the little sloop **SQUIRREL** out of Gloucester, Andrew Haraden, commander. Haraden testified in Boston that, *"the day after I was taken, pirate crewman John Filmore, declared his mind to me, to rise upon the Pyrates in order to subdue them. . . . Edward Cheesman* (a pirate), *upon the rising, threw John Nutt, the Master of the Pyrates overboard, and John Filmore struck Burrell the boatswain on the head with a broad axe, while I and the others dispatched Captain Philip and the others. . . Philip and Burrell's heads were brought into Boston in pickle"* — Haraden had chopped their heads off and preserved them in vinegar. Pirate John Nutt, who drowned, had been one of Blackbeard's crewmen. Because of their help in the uprising, pirates Cheesman and Filmore were found not guilty of piracy, as were 10 of the others who helped Haraden capture the pirate ship. Four, including William Phillips, were found guilty and three were hanged. Haraden's grandson, Jon Haraden, became the greatest privateersman in America during the Revolutionary War, and pirate John Filmore's great grandson became the 13th President of the United States — Millard Filmore.

Two pirates who used the Isles of Shoals as a base of operation were the Walls, a man and wife team. Rachel Wall was a Beacon Hill maid in Boston and her husband George was a fisherman who served as a sailor aboard a privateer during the Revolution. Stealing a sloop at Essex, with a pirate crew of four men, the Walls moved to Appledore Island, pretending to be a fishing family. Indeed, they did fish now and then, but using an old trick of Ned Low's, they induced vessels to come to them while at sea, by flying a distress-flag. During the Summers of 1781 and 82, they took twelve vessels, robbing, then murdering the crews, and sinking the ships. With the distress-flag flying, Rachel would stand by the mast, waving on the captains and crews intent on saving her. She would scream for help until they came alongside, and then they were bludgeoned and stabbed by George and his pals. In all, some 24 men were murdered and over $6,000 collected in cash. Plus, the pirates gained money from the supplies these would-be rescue ships were carrying, which they confiscated and later sold at Boston and Portsmouth.

The missing ships and crewmen were considered lost at sea in storms and the pirates were never caught. In September of 1782, however, with distress-flag flying, the Wall's vessel encountered a hurricane. George Wall and one of the crewmen were washed overboard and Rachel, with the three other pirates, had to really be rescued.

Rachel Wall retired from the sea and went back to being a maid for the wealthy Brahmins of Beacon Hill. As a hobby, she continued robbing by visiting the vessels at dockside in Boston Harbor and taking money and trinkets from any unlocked cabins. In September, 1789, at age 29, she was caught red-handed in a cabin, and aboard the ship, constables found a dead sailor. Rachel was accused of murdering the seaman in his bunk, which, to her dying day, she swore she didn't do. None-the-less, she was tried and convicted, and sentenced to hang on Boston Common on October 8, 1789. Before the noose was placed around her neck, she confessed to being a pirate. Yet, she was not hanged for piracy, but for a murder she didn't commit— Rachel was the last woman to be executed in the state of Massachusetts, and the last known pirate to work out of the Isles of Shoals.

Nix's Mate Island in Boston Harbor, near Deer Island, Winthrop, where pirates were hanged, gibbeted, and buried. The 13 acre island sank after an innocent man was hanged there for piracy, and only this 32-foot high pyramid, topped with a beacon, remains today. Nearby at Deer Island, treasure hunters search for buried treasure near the seawall, where 1,200 silver Mexican dollars were dug up in 1906.

VI
TAKE THE LOW ROAD

"You take the high road and I"ll take the low road," the old Scottish song goes, but taking either road in New England could bring you a fortune once you reach the end of it— if you bring a good metal-detector with you, and have a pretty good idea where to search to find buried treasure. I was on one of the high roads treasure hunting for three days recently, with famed *"coin-shooter"* (metal-detecting expert) Al Janard. We hunted an old 19th century picnic ground near Wilmont-Flat, New Hampshire, where Al uncovered over 90 silver and copper coins, and I came home with but four Indian-head pennies. Al is obviously a better treasure hunter than I am. He prefers hunting the uplands of New Hampshire and Vermont, and I prefer to take the low road, in search of the more exciting, yet elusive pirate treasures. The islands and coastal area of Rhode Island and the Isles of Shoals, New Hampshire, as thus far indicated, are prime areas for searching and finding buried pirate loot, as are the islands and inlets of Maine and Massachusetts. Al Janard, my wife Sandy, and Jim Whittall— founder of the Early Sites Research Society — recently searched Bar Head, Plum Island, at Newburyport, Massachusetts because others searching before us had found ancient Roman coins and 18th century Spanish gold doubloons there, all within the past six years. We came up empty handed.

At Ipswich, Salisbury and nearby Hampton Beach, New Hampshire, old Spanish pieces-of-eight, all dated around 1715, are constantly being dug up in the sand. One uncovered by Al Janard at Ipswich, was dated 1732. Many good treasure spots are never revealed however, for the finders want to protect their own little nest-eggs. A good example of this is the sand-pocket one-half mile up Marconi Beach, Wellfleet, Massachusetts, that was first revealed in newspapers in 1982, when Barry Clifford found the wreck of the 1717 pirate ship **WHYDAH**. Prior to that, beachcombers would pluck silver pieces-of-eight at the same spot after every wild Northeast storm, keeping their finds and this lucrative location a deep dark secret. Cape Codders Asa Cole and Henry Daniels had picked up some 300 silver coins there over the years, without divulging the source of their riches. Race Point, Provincetown, Nauset Beach, and Chatham Dunes are other known spots at Cape Cod for finding 18th century silver coins washed in from shipwrecks, or possibly from some pirate cache buried deep in the sand.

Fisherman Arthur Doane found $60,000 in gold coins near Chatham Light in the late 1800's, supposedly from a treasure chest buried there by pirates. Before Doane died, he revealed to relatives that he didn't dig out all the gold, for a storm had covered it over, and about twenty-five percent of it remains buried in the sand. In January of 1934, Earl Rich of Yarmouth dug up a clay pot of silver coins and two pirate cutlasses at Great Island, Cape Cod. One of the cutlasses has the date *"1703"* scratched into it.

The islands off Cape Cod should uncover pirate caches for the dedicated treasure hunter as well, especially Elizabeth Islands — Cuttyhunk and Nashaun Islands in particular— for pirates were known to anchor often in Tarpoulin Cove. These islands are still pretty well desolated, and had to be choice spots for pirates to bank their wealth. A man and wife pirate team, Eric and Maria Cobham, active in the 1700s, supposedly buried their gold on Nantucket Island, and two 19th century pirates named Johnson and Walker, admitted to burying treasure at Martha's Vineyard. Walker, a mate aboard the Salem brig **SPLENDID**, poisoned his captain John Harding, and transfered 60,000 silver dollars in canvas bags from the **SPLENDID** to Pirate Captain Johnson's ship, the **MARY ALICE**. Johnson, in 1846, buried his half share of the treasure at the beach near East Chop Light. Walker also buried his 30,000 pieces of silver at Martha's Vineyard, but later, while moving his treasure to bury it on the mainland in Falmouth, he was captured. His share of the treasure was confiscated by the Sheriff. Johnson, hearing of Walker's capture, fled New England, and never dared return for his share of the silver. Supposedly, it remains buried in the sand.

Three children started a gold rush at Edgewater Beach, Hull, Massachusetts, in 1967, after finding old coins in the sand. Stephen Doyle (age 11) and his sister Julie (age six) first uncovered a wooden box in the shallows while wading, and with it, a sealed leather pouch. They gathered up 70 coins of silver and gold, most dating in the early 1700s, and some were extremely rare. Word spread like wild-fire, and hundreds of locals, carrying shovels and metal-detectors, scoured the beach, but only a few more coins were found. Across Boston Harbor from Hull, near Nix's Mate Island, 18th century Mexican coins, some 1,200 of them, were found at Deer Island, Winthrop, in October of 1906. Also, in 1880, a gold-rush like that in Hull was ignited at Winthrop. Dan Duffield, age 12, found a ripped canvas bag half filled with silver and gold coins on Short Beach after a storm. They were Mexican and Spanish coins, dated in the 19th century, from 1822 to 1835. Over 100 people came to search the sand, and over 1,000 coins were uncovered, but whether they came from an offshore wreck or a buried treasure, nobody knows. Similar coins are periodically found at Short Beach and

Grover's Cliff, as well as at neighboring Nahant and Revere. Skindiving in the shallows at Bass Point, Nahant, Art Channell of Beverly recently found a Spanish medallion. Mendal Peterson of the Smithsonian Institute, after studying the medallion, indicated that it may have come from the same treasure load that was found at Winthrop in 1880 and at Deer Island in 1906.

Further up the North Shore of Massachusetts at Ipswich, an 1880 diary records that coins similar to those found at Winthrop were uncovered *"by several Essex men who were gunning on Ipswich Beach."* Mr. Proctor, the diarist, writes, *"they picked up several Mexican dollars, and on the following day, three more were found... They were believed to come from the brig FALCONER that was cast away off Castle Neck on December 17th, 1847... About thirty Essex young men armed with hoes, shovels and rakes went to the spot and searched for treasure, but to no avail."* Similar coins have been found by hunters with metaldetectors at Crane's Beach and Little Neck, Ipswich within the last few years. Also, rumor has it that clam diggers recently found six silver bars in the mudflats at Essex.

An illusive pirate treasure has been searched for on the banks of the Parker River at nearby Byfield, for over sixty-four years, but to no avail. A wooden chest, covered with thick leather, bound with copper straps, containing over $200,000 in gold and silver coins, was shipped almost half way around the world, from 1799 through 1800, until it landed in Massachusetts. It was the property of Captain Roger Hayman, commander of some 400 pirates who infested the Caribbean in the late 18th century. His headquarters on the island of Haiti was attacked by the American Navy on December 31, 1799, and although Hayman, with a fleet of ten pirate vessels, sailed out to battle the warships, six of his fleet were destroyed by the schooner **EXPERIMENT** and the frigate **BOSTON**. Hayman, however, badly wounded, managed to escape in his ship. He sailed for England, where he disbanded his pirate crew. Hoping to find protection with his family in Bristol, he was told that they had moved to New York in his absence. Still suffering from his wounds, he boarded a passenger ship to New York at Liverpool, under an alias. His trunks, filled with the treasure he had collected over the years, were safely stored with him in his cabin.

An English doctor named Griffen who was aboard, was called to Hayman's cabin shortly after they were underway. Hayman's wounds were festering and he was feverish. Before Griffen would treat him, he made the pirate confess to how he could have possibly received such severe wounds. By the time the ship reached Newburyport, the first stop before sailing on to New York, Hayman was in a coma and Doctor Griffen was sure that he would soon die. The doctor had befriended another passenger aboard the ship, a New Yorker named Sterns Compton. While in port, he persuaded Compton to remove one of the chests from Hayman's cabin, and load it onto a dock-side wagon. Hiring the wagon, Griffen and Compton left the ship and headed south. With darkness setting in, they got only as far as Putnam Tavern on the Boston-Newburyport Road, where they decided to stay the night.

While eating breakfast at the tavern next morning, a man arrived from Newburyport to announce to all in the tavern that the *"constables and sherriff's men were out looking for two men who stole a considerable sum of money from a purser's safe of a ship docked at the port."* Trying to look as inconspicuous as possible, the two robbers gulped their food and headed the wagon down a side road toward the Parker River. There, they nervously decided to break open the chest, take as many coins as they could comfortably carry, and hide the rest somewhere nearby. They swore an oath to each other that they would not return for the bulk of the treasure until the Fourth of July, 1806. Inside the locked trunk they found canvas bags filled with gold and silver coins, and took as many as they could carry. Then, they buried or hid the remaining treasure nearby, and rode on to Boston.

It wasn't until 1923, that anyone knew about the treasure at Byfield, or that neither Doctor Griffen nor Sterns Compton, ever returned to further divide the treasure. Both had wisely invested the money they had carried into New York. By 1806, they were wealthy beyond their dreams. Griffen contacted Compton before the July 4th deadline, and they agreed to leave well enough alone. They didn't need the money, nor were they willing to risk going back for it. Before Compton died in 1857, he told his family about the pirate treasure, and in 1923, his great-granddaughter came to Byfield hoping to find it, *"hidden under a rock on the banks of the river. The rock being marked with a letter 'A',"* her ancestor had informed the family, but she couldn't find it. After a few weeks of searching, she left Byfield, but told a family living there that she would share the treasure with them if they could find it— they couldn't. In 1943, however, a Byfield farmer, digging a well near the river, uncovered a few Spanish coins, dated 1794. Whether these were from Pirate Hayman's chest, no one knows, nor is the farmer willing to discuss the matter further.

Although 20th century coin-shooters are quite secretive about what they find and where they hunt, information on where people have accidentally stumbled upon pirate loot in the 19th century, is readily available in old newspapers. Small caches of pirate treasure stored in canvas bags, iron kettles, boxes, and clay pots, buried and forgotten, or never retrieved because of premature death, which was a common occurrence among pirates, have been dug up periodically along the New England Coast. One such find usually begets another, for pirate crews often left their ships together to bury their personal shares of booty ashore in the same general area. Tuxis Island near Milford, Connecticut should be a good hunting ground, for in 1903, a group of boys, from the Y.M.C.A. camp located there, found a great quantity of 18th century coins and some gold jewelry buried in the sand. The beach near Penfield Reef, Fairfield, Connecticut, should be another key coin-shooting spot. This is where, in 1888, George Hawley dug up a cache of gold and silver coins dated 1795, thought to have been buried by a pirate earlier in that century.

Also, places that pirates were known to frequent, like Portsmouth, New Hampshire, Kittery, Castine, and Damariscotta, Maine, are locations that are bound to eventually turn up pirate treasure — Damariscove Island is a place that should be visited by hunters with metaldetectors, and I would be surprised if they left that island empty handed. Casco Bay is another ripe spot in Maine. At the Cedar Ledges, east of Ram Island in Casco Bay, John Wilson of Orr Island accidentally stumbled upon three kettles of Spanish silver coins on Thanksgiving Day, 1852. Wilson bought two houses, two ships, and 100 acres of woodland with the money he got when he sold his pirate coins. Three years later, farmer Richard Hanscom while plowing a field, dug up a large treasure of gold and silver in earthen pots at Richmond Island, south of Cape Elizabeth. He donated most of the treasure to the Maine Historical Society, valued today at about $800,000. At Harpswell Neck, a lobsterman found $2,000 in buried pirate money in a clay jar, uncovered in the sand by a storm in 1870. Thirty years earlier, fisherman John Wilson found a kettle of gold coins buried in the flats between Reef Ram Island and Elm Island, Maine. Penobscot Bay is another good place to search for pirate loot. A hermit, known only as Harry, lived on Criehaven Island. He readily showed visitors who came to the island the pirate treasure he had dug up there, until one day Harry disappeared along with his treasure. This Island was called *"Racketash"* by the Indians, but is often referred to as *"Ragged Arse"* by today's Penobscot natives. At nearby Codhead Marsh, on the Penobscot River, a group of boys uncovered a cache of pirate coins, all dated 1798 and 1799. The six-mile-long Isle Au Haut was also a pirate hangout, and is peppered with caves to hide treasure in. The island once had over 800 inhabitants, but the lore of gold drove them away — the San Francisco Gold Rush of

1849 reduced the island population to 42.

Probably the richest treasure, found accidentally in Maine, was that discovered on the banks of the Bagaduce River at Castine in 1840. Stephen Grindle was clearing trees near Johnson's Narrows on an old Indian path, when he uncovered six Spanish pieces-of-eight. Unfortunately it was starting to snow, and Grindle had to wait for the snow to clear to search for more coins. When the ground thawed, he started digging, and found over 700 Portuguese, Spanish and French silver and gold coins, and a few were Indian and Chinese. Most were dated in the 17th century. Thought to be a pirate treasure, it could have been French Baron Castine's hoard, purposely buried by him when the British invaded his trading post in the late 1600's. He died destitute in France a few years later. Be it Baron Castine's hidden treasure, or that of one of the pirate chiefs, Grindle wasn't really aware of its value, for he started spending it — piece by piece — at the local grocery store for food and tobacco. Finally a coin dealer caught up with him and Stephen sold his treasure, which was worth well over a million dollars.

The story of the last pirate hanged in New England involves my home town of Salem, Massachusetts and it also has an indirect moral for treasure hunters. The brig MEXICAN of Salem, Captain John Butman, commander, was off Cuba in 1832, when approached by the Spanish yacht PANDA. Captain of the PANDA was Don Pedro Gilbert, and with him were 30 pirates. The MEXICAN had two cannons for defense but, as the helmsman reported, *"our means of defense proved utterly worthless, as the shot was a number of sizes too large for the guns."* The pirates easily took the MEXICAN as their prize and found ten large chests of silver that was her cargo.

"Armed with swords and clubs, the buccaneers unmercifully beat our men," writes helmsman John Battis, *"then they locked us all below and torched the ship."* As the PANDA sailed off with the chests of silver, the MEXICAN crew managed to break down the cabin door, get up on deck, and put out the fire. She returned to Salem on October 12, 1832, and the Essesx Register published an account of the incident. Months later, Captain Hunt of Salem, anchored off St. Thomas in the West Indies, while reading a copy of the Essex Register, with the pirating report in it, looked up to see the PANDA coming into port. Hunt notified the commander of a British man-of-war, CURLEW that was also in port. The PANDA, was pursued and sunk, and the commander with nine pirate crewmen were captured. They were delivered as prisoners to Salem, and immediately taken to Old Town Hall where they were given a hearing. Present were the MEXICAN

captain and crew, ready to testify against the PANDA captain and crew who had not only robbed and beaten them, but tried to burn them alive. Thomas Fuller, a MEXICAN crewman, when called on to identify pirate Francisco Ruiz — the one who had beaten him with a club, instead broke the pirate's jaw with a punch to the face.

Not able to conduct a fair trial in Salem, the pirates were transfered to Boston. The only pirate of the PANDA found innocent was the first mate, Bernard DeSoto. Years before, De Soto had saved 70 seamen from Salem when the ship MINERVA was shipwrecked in the West Indies, and the people of Salem had awarded him a silver cup for bravery. President Andrew Jackson gave De Soto a pardon and shipped him back to Spain. Judge Joseph Story, also a Salem boy, pronounced the sentence of death by hanging for the others. Two of the pirates attempted suicide while awaiting execution and one succeeded. The other was so weakened by the attempt on his own life that he had to sit in a chair at the gallows. On March 11, 1835, six of the PANDA pirates, including Captain Gilbert were hanged. Francisco Ruiz could not be hanged, according to law, for he had gone insane. Still mentally deranged eleven months later, the court decided to hang him anyway. Ruiz was the last pirate executed in New England.

Francisco Ruiz's *"life long obsession with gold and silver,"* so the judge claimed, *"caused him to go insane,"* and his greed brought him eventually to the gallows.

I have seen that fizzled, crazy look in people's eyes when they see pirate treasure — and hunting for it can be as addictive as drugs. I once had a friend who decided to hunt full time for treasure. He first lost a lucrative business, then his house, and then his wife — and he never found a penny. The moral is, don't go crazy searching for pirate treasure. Take your time, research as best you can, pursue your leads in your spare time and, above all, have fun. Good hunting !